Sleep Never Comes For Th

Did Not Rea

Part One

****

Author Pam McCagh

These Are Their Stories, And This

Is Their Book.

I am sitting here thinking, how will I tell you all about the book? There are so many spirit people involved that I feel honoured to tell some of their stories. Where do I begin?

First, I must tell you that the stories you read are their stories. They have been written as they speak. I find myself sitting in a chair and feel the line of people queuing behind me to tell their stories.

The first thing I have to do is to write the title. Then, I find myself automatically writing. That means sitting and listening to what they say and then writing it down. I sit until the story has finished. Each story normally takes twenty minutes to one hour.

I have had many happy hours working with them, and I hope that by reading this book, you will feel the love and compassion for those who did not reach the other fifty-four stories that have been completed.

The front page has been designed by the spirits themselves. Everything in this book has been the inspiration of the spirit world.

Table Of Contents

Table Of Contents

Dedications

This book is dedicated to my friend Fred. Fred is my guide and best friend. I want to thank my husband, Paul, for the love and patience he gave to me while I was writing this book.

To my son Paul, thank you for all his hard work and support. He was always there for me, and Amanda Donnelly for editing and proofreading.

1. The Coal Miner's Son

I had just finished telling Robbie to go further down and that I was coming behind him. It was pitch black, and we couldn't see a foot ahead of us. All of a sudden, there was a big rumble of noise and an explosion. I reached out to Robbie but could not find him. I called his name and stepped forward, feeling my arms outstretched. Then there was nothing. I heard screams. I felt something against my foot, and I reached down to see what it was. I could feel someone's clothing. I found his face. Oh God, it's Robbie! I pulled him as close as I could, but I couldn't get him to stand up. I sat down and pulled him towards me. His body was very limp, and I held him in my arms. I asked him time and time again. "Please answer me"', but there was nothing. I cradled him in my arms and thought, someone will find us soon. I looked around, but there was only darkness. I pulled him closer to me and rocked him. I thought of long ago when he was just a baby.

As soon as I came home from work and opened the door, he was there, hanging on to my trouser leg. I would pick him up, throw him into the air and give him that special little look. He's a lot bigger now.

I remember the day he told me he was going into the mines. I told him, "Over my dead body." As usual, he did not listen. I told him that my father and his father before him had always worked underground. I told him I had lost both my father and my grandfather, but like all kids, he did not listen.

It was about the time when all miners were having it hard. It had been six weeks, and things were not getting any better. Mother had spent the little money she had, which was only pennies.

She said we would neither borrow nor lend any money. She was a very proud woman, my Annie. Things got worse. We were lucky we only had one son. We had a lot of trouble after our first son was born, and the doctor said no more children. We loved our son very much and did not want him to go underground.

I remember my father saying, "Don't let it happen", but we were living on raw potatoes now, and things could not get any worse. Then one of the Gaffers said, "We need someone to crawl under the face. Because your Robbie is small, we will give him the job. We can only pay him five pennies." I said no to the Gaffer, but he said Robbie only had to go down three times. With so much hunger around, I finally gave in.

Robbie went down. I could see from the look on his face that the first time he came back up, he was petrified. We begged him not to go down again. But his silly pride got in the way, and down he went, and that was the beginning. He said he would only do it for a year or so until we got back on our feet.

One year turned into two. The second year he had been going down, his mother said a friend of hers was coming to visit from the next town, which was only fifteen miles from Hull.

She arrived the following day late in the evening. She brought with her two small children and a girl. We looked at them with pity. They looked as though they had had no food for months. We told them to sit by the fire and get warm.

The oldest lass was called Bonnie. I saw Robbie looking from the corner of his eye. I smiled. He was coming into eighteen now. He was no longer a boy. It was good for the missus to have a bit of company.

She started to laugh again. Young Bonnie would help her with the cleaning and washing. Then, one day, Robbie asked permission to take Bonnie to see the fairground. Mum's friend Aggie said that was fine, and that's how it all began.

Six months went by, and Robbie and Bonnie were married.

It wasn't a posh do, but Bonnie looked great. They looked so proud. Aggie had already left a few months before but came back again for the wedding. She still looked very sick. Her husband had no work. We put everything behind us for that one special day. I was so proud; we danced until late.

Robbie and Bonnie had to have a spare bedroom. It was not a bedroom, really, just a small place big enough to put a bed in, but it was theirs.

It only seemed a couple of months had passed when Bonnie said she was expecting a baby. They both smiled, and I could not believe my ears. At that time, I had my old work boots in my hand. I threw them so high into the sky that one of them came down and hit me on the head. Everyone laughed.

Later that night, I asked Robbie to come for a walk. We walked together for a while. I said I wanted him and Bonnie to leave Hull when the baby was born and find a better life. He said he was happy here with Mother and me. I told him that people did not live long working underground.

He said, "You have." I said, "Yes, but your mother has to live every day of her life wondering when I go down, will I ever come back up? And I don't want that for you and Bonnie." He said he would talk to Bonnie that night, and he did.

The following day, Bonnie said, "When the baby is six weeks old, we will leave." She looked at Robbie with sad eyes and said, "I don't want to be one of those wives who pray every day for their husbands to come back up."

So the decision had been made, and we were all so happy. Bonnie had only a few weeks to go, and we were excited. Time slipped back. As I held my son in my arms, I knew that he would never live to see his child grow up. My heart ached. I could feel his body, cold and wet, as I held him even closer.

It was pitch black, and there was no sound. I called out, "Is there anyone there? If there is a God, then let it be now. Let my son and me get out of this bloody mess." I lay back on the wall, and I felt nothing. I realised that there was blood running from my head onto the side of my shoulder and down onto Robbie; that's why Robbie was so wet.

I lay my head back and asked once again, "Please help us." Then I heard a voice from beside me asking me to put my light on. The switch was on my helmet, and I said I couldn't reach it and that the battery had failed.

The voice said again, "Reach up and turn on your light." I did, and the light came on. The light was on the front of my helmet, so when I turned my head around, the light would follow.

I gently turned my head to the left and then to the right. In a split second, the light caught something. I turned my head back to where it was, and a small light appeared. It was so beautiful and tiny that when the lights flicked on it, it looked like a small hole in the wall.

I had never seen anything so beautiful in my life; so many beautiful colours that I did not recognise from this world. They were getting brighter now, and it seemed to fill the whole shaft. I took a deep breath. For the first time, I felt wonderful and free.

The voice told me and Robbie to stand up. I don't know why, but I obeyed.

As I got up, I felt Robbie standing up with me. Robbie looked at me and said, "We'll be alright now, won't we, Dad?" I said, "Yes, Son." Then we walked together through the face of the shaft and into the light.

2. Who Will Tell My Wife?

I lay here thinking, who will tell my wife I won't be coming home? Who will tell her how much I love her? I will never see my unborn child. I am starting to lose my eyesight. It must be around two o'clock. The sun is still high in the sky. I turn my head around, and I can see Smithy. He's not moving. I call his name, and he still does not answer. God, what's happening? I turn around the other way. I can see James - we all call him Jimmy. He does not like James. We used to laugh about it when things were different.

I am getting colder now. I shout, "Where's the Medic?" I can still hear Jimmy breathing. Where's that medic? I no longer feel my legs. I listen again to the sound of gunshots, and I can still hear the blokes fighting. I don't think they are far away, but it could be miles. Can't anyone find us? Jimmy needs help now! Jimmy's the youngest one in our platoon. We used to joke with him, calling him our baby boy. We should have told him how much we loved and respected him. Now, it may be too late. I called Jimmy again but still got no answer.

It rained last night. We're lying in a puddle of mud. My mind is drifting now, remembering my wife, Patsy. Everyone has a memory of something; mine was when Patsy used to bake. I used to watch those programs where the women used to get flour all over their hair and noses. Patsy would beat that. She would get the flour all over the kitchen walls and the floor. That's my memory of my Patsy.

I received a letter two weeks ago saying I will be a Daddy. I was so proud of her. Oh God, who is going to tell her? I can hear someone shouting in the background. I try to lift my hand up, but I can't. My memories go back again to Patsy. Where is she now? And what is she doing? I put a picture of her in my mind. Oh God, she's so beautiful.

Before I joined the army, we would go to the pictures every Friday night, and on Saturday, we would help her Mum and Dad. Her dad had been very sick, so I would help with the heavy jobs around the farm. The old man had a few cows, three maybe, a couple of sheep and a few chooks, and an old goat that must be dead by now. How long has it been since I joined up? It has been two years.

I hear Jimmy making a noise with his hand. He's trying to reach mine, but he can't reach it. I can see a stick. If I can reach it, I can give it to Jimmy to hold so he doesn't feel so lonely. I've nearly got it now. I'm holding on tight to it. I reach out towards Jimmy. I can feel him holding on to the stick. Oh God, what's happening? He's shaking so bloody hard. I can't hold on any longer. I try to call out to him, but my voice doesn't come through. I try to lift my fingers so he knows I'm OK. I can see him looking towards me, but now he's just staring. I shout, but no words come out. Where's that bloody Medic? I can feel myself drifting into darkness.

I'm at home again with my brother and sister. I can hear the kettle boiling. I shout to my mother, "The kettle's boiling, Mum!" She calls back, "Can you turn it off? I'm just hanging the washing out." It's been a long day for me. I've been working in the fields logging, and there is no rest between times of felling. I look at my hands; they have blisters from cutting the timber. I rub a bit of goose fat on. It smarts for a moment, and then it feels good.

I call out to Mum, "Will Dad be home tonight?" She replies, "No, Son, he's thirty miles away. I don't expect him for a few days yet." My friend Bobby calls, "Coming for a ride, Pete?" I quickly jumped in beside him, and off we went to the old Woodstock, where I met my beautiful Patsy. We were married within that year, and then the bad news came of the war. Six months later, I was called up.

I felt myself back in the fields with my mates, and reality came flooding back.

I look across, but Jimmy's still starring at me. I think he's gone. Where's the bloody medic? I stand up and look down, and there are the three of us, so still. Someone tugs at my arm and says, "Come on, mate. Let's go."

3. The Sergeant And His Men

I lay with my arms outstretched. I felt someone grab hold of my hand. It was very cold. I asked, "Is someone there?" The answer came very quickly, "Yes." I immediately saw a man in uniform, and then he slowly sat down by my side. He looked very tired and confused. I asked if he needed help. He looked at me with so much sadness. "Yes, I do, but I can't leave my men."

I looked to where he was pointing and saw eleven very broken men. Some of them had homemade crutches with bandages on their heads and legs; some could not see and relied on the other soldier in front to guide them. Their uniforms were torn and tattered, and all were very lost within themselves.

I felt the pain that they were carrying. I looked back at the soldier still holding my hand and said,

"It's up to you now." He said, "How?" I told him to get up and that he was a disgrace to his uniform. He immediately stood up and started to tidy up his appearance. He looked at me for approval; I told him the rest was now up to him. He took a deep breath and took command like any good soldier. He called out. "Get up, you lazy layabouts!" As he watched, his men slowly got to their feet in confusion. With the next breath, he shouted, "Straighten your uniforms; you are a disgrace to your country!" I smiled as I watched each man straighten his uniform and look at the Sergeant with greater respect.

He took up a salute, and in return, the men saluted him back. He called out, "Right about turn!" and marched forward with his men, holding their heads high. I was told to walk by his side until someone came for him and his mates.

The Sergeant said, "I can feel the warmth on my face; it feels good." The other men shouted to me, too.

I looked back to see them smiling from ear to ear. I was told to stop and let them go. As I watched, it was something that I would remember for the rest of my life. The soldiers dropped their walking aids, took off their bandages and walked together like new men. The light was getting brighter now.

I saw the last man walk past the Sergeant with pride. He turned, smiled at me, saluted me with great care and then turned back and marched after his men. I smiled all the way back home.

4. To Whom It May Concern

I should have written this letter about sixty-eight years ago, but when you're young, you don't quite understand what is happening. When you are older, you are afraid to know.

We were brought up in the city. Mum had a brother who lived in the country. Now and again, he would invite us all to stay. It was a huge house with seven or eight bedrooms and just as many living rooms, if not more. We had visited him quite a few times.

One day, my Uncle said someone had moved in next door, and she would be around my age. Would I like to call over to meet her? I said, "Yes, please." I was nine years old.

Uncle Dave took me next door to introduce us to the family. She had dark hair and huge glasses. She would have been the same age as me. We were a bit strange with each other at first, but we soon became friends.

Then, one day, we played hide and seek. We played it a few times, and then I decided that I would make it hard for her to find me. I climbed the staircase to the top room and hid there. I waited for a long time, but she could not find me.

As I was leaving the room, I heard someone laughing. I looked around, but there was no one in the room. The laughter seemed to come from the floorboards. I bent down, and I could see through a small hole. Uncle Dave was on top of this young girl, and they were laughing together.

I thought I'd better go down and find my new friend. Just at that moment, I thought I'd heard a scream. I went down the stairs to find my friend. She said, "Where have you been? I've been looking all over for you." I said I was sorry. We played other games, and then it was time for me to go back home.

I was only home for a few days when Mum got sick. Uncle Dave said I could stay with him for a couple of weeks. I thought good, I was glad to be back again.

I went to see Uncle Dave. He was sorry, but he had to go out the following morning; would I be okay on my own? I said, "Yes."When I got up, he had already left.

I wandered around for a while and then returned to the top bedroom. I looked out of the window and could see everything around me. Then I heard the laughing again.

I thought to myself, Uncle Dave said he was not going to come back until late afternoon. I looked down through the floorboards again, and there he was, with another girl. I remember thinking he was very kind to the girls, and he always made them laugh.

By the time I went back home, three other girls had been in. I don't know why, but I never thought to ask who they were. I was too busy looking around the rooms. Then, one day, Mother said I could not go to see Uncle Dave again,

I never thought any more about it until one day when Mother and I were shopping, I picked up a newspaper and saw two, maybe three, of the girls that I had seen at Uncle Dave's house. I asked Mother what had happened to these girls. She said to put the paperback and don't ask questions.

I was thinking of the girls all day. I thought I should go and tell Mother. When I tried to ask her again about the girls, she bit my head off and said, "I've got to go now. I will be back at nine o'clock", and was going through the door.

I thought of those young girls many times after that, but no one seemed to want to hear what I was saying, so I just forgot about them.

Then, many years later, I made friends with a really nice woman next door. Her name was Ann. We were both in our late sixties now, and we used to talk about what we did when we were children.

Ann told me that she had a sister. I asked where she was. Ann said she had died a long time ago, that her body had been found in the bushes. When I asked what bushes, she told me Palmer's Spring bush. That was a piece of land that used to belong to the Palmer family. I asked her what happened. Ann told me she had been murdered.

I did not think any more of it until a few weeks later when Ann asked me around for tea, and I saw a picture of a young girl. I asked who she was, and Ann said that it was her sister who had died. I caught my breath and thought to myself, that was the young girl I saw laughing that day at my uncle's house. I could not forget about it.

As time went by, I found out a little bit more. I eventually discovered what had happened to the other two young girls and thought, what a silly young girl I was. Why didn't I tell someone?

I remembered trying to tell Mother, but like all grownups, she did not want to listen. I thought long and hard about it and then decided to write this letter.

I leaned back in my chair, and I was feeling very tired. I remember thinking, what a silly old fool I've been. I should have done this a long time ago.

When I opened my eyes again, there were strange people in my house. I saw my friend Ann crying and wondered what had happened to make her so upset. I looked around the room, and everything was still in its place.

Then I looked at the chair and saw myself asleep. I could not believe what I was seeing. Am I going mad, I thought? Are my old eyes deceiving me? Then I heard the doctor saying, "She died in her sleep." I put my hand to my mouth. I couldn't believe the words that I was hearing. They left the room and went into the kitchen.

I sat there thinking, what had I done? What a silly old fool I am. I saw the letter tucked neatly into a book. If I had thought about it, I could have left the letter there in the open for someone to find it.

I sat there for a time, watching things happening and not being able to communicate with anyone. I saw my friend bend down and kiss my forehead, and I thought if I could only move the book, she might find the letter.

I don't know how I did it, but I knocked the book off the little table. She picked up the book and was just about to place it back on the table, but she read the front of the book, which said, "To my Friend."

It was a strange feeling, but I heard what she was thinking. She thought that as she picked up the book, my friend would not mind if I took the book that she was holding before she passed away. She clutched the book in her hands and walked out of the door. I tried to follow her, but it felt like someone had put a glass cage around the house. I couldn't get out. I watched her through the window, tapping it and thinking, please read the book.

I don't know how long I'd been there, and it seemed like a long time, maybe two or three days, watching people come in, checking the house and taking my body away. People were using my phone, thinking that there was no one there to see.

It must have been a week later when my friend Ann walked back in. She looked around with a strange look in her eye. I noticed straight away she was clutching the book. She stood there in front of the chair where she had last seen me and said, "I know you are still in this house somewhere.

I know that you moved the book so that I could find your letter and I am very grateful to you. You see, I could never close the book on my sister's death. Now you have told me everything I needed to know in your letter. I took the letter to the police station, and they confirmed other things for me. I can now leave my sister to rest in peace

.I know you can hear me, and I am grateful to you for having the courage to write the letter. I do understand that when you were small, nobody wanted to listen. I also had the same problem. I saw a photograph once of your uncle and my sister, but I was brushed off.

They said it was part of a family photo. Now I know the difference. So, God bless you, my friend, and I know we will meet again soon. Go now and find your peace".With that, she walked out of the door.

I followed her all the way down the path and through the gate. I felt the freedom that I'd never felt before, and I heard Mother calling me.

5. The Whisperer

The car was packed to the hilt; the dog and two kids were in the back. We were just coming around the corner when one of the boys shouted, "There it is, Mommy! It's over there!" He was so excited, and there, coming into view, was the house that we bought through the paper. It read, "Secluded, with beautiful gardens, close to shops and schools". It looked so beautiful in the picture, with timber floors and tall trees all around.

We had come from a huge town. When the divorce became final, I thought it would be good for the boys and me to have a bit of country life away from all the wagging tongues. The closer we got to the house, the more disappointed we were. It was quite rundown; there were no flowers to speak of, and part of the picket fence had been torn down. The "For Sale" sign was still standing.

We all got out of the car, and little Jimmy put his hands on his hips and said, "Man, this house is really old, isn't it?" I just stood there looking at it. "Well, it is", I said, "but it's all we have for the moment. Let's look inside." We opened the gate, and it fell out of my hands and onto the ground.

We walked up to the door and pushed it open gently. We walked inside, and my youngest son, Richard, said, "Hey, Man, this is fun, isn't it?" I looked down at him, touched his hair, and said, "Yes, darling." We walked through to the kitchen, and I thought, Wow! It had windows all around, an old gas stove and a sink that belonged in the past.

I left the children to look around and went back to the car for some boxes. Jimmy came out to help and said, "Are we really going to stay and live here?" I said, "Yes, darling, for the time being."

I had just started to unpack the car when a car pulled up. A woman stepped out, and the first thing I noticed was her boots. They were orange, and as she stepped out of the car, I thought, this lady likes a lot of colour.

She came over to me, shook my hand, and said, "Hi there, my name is Betsy." I looked at her, and she didn't wait for an answer. She just walked straight into the old house into the kitchen and put the kettle on.

She brought some coffee, sugar and cups out of her pocket. I wondered if she had anything else tucked in her skirt with those huge pockets. She went back to the car and brought back a tin. She said, "I've got cookies." We all stood, flabbergasted.

She said to us, Come on, sit down and have a drink and a cookie." We all did as we were told. It took her five minutes to drink and eat, and then she was out of the door, bringing in our cases and boxes. She would have been seventy or a little more, but she had so much energy.

The car and the trailer had been emptied in less than half-hour. I smiled and said, "Thank you so much." She said she would call again tomorrow to see if we wanted anything, and then she was gone. The next morning, she was knocking on the window. I looked at the clock; it was only half-past seven.

She let herself in, rolling her sleeves up and scrubbing the kitchen tops spotless. She talked all the time about her Henry. I didn't get a chance to ask her who he was; she just went from one room to another, cleaning, tidying, and polishing.

At lunchtime, I made a quick salad, and we all sat at the table. She said it was so good to have us here. I asked where she lived, and she replied, "Five miles down the road." I asked her how long she had been living here. She said she was born here, and her mother and grandmother were born here.

Next week, she said, she would take the boys hunting. The boys' heads shot up, and both looked at me. She asked them if they had been hunting before. They sat there and shook their heads from side to side. "I have two small rifles.

I will clean them tonight, and next week, we will go looking for bears", she said with a big grin. She never asked if I would let them go. She slapped me on my shoulder and said, "I look forward to seeing you all tomorrow." Then off she went. This went on for two months. I was beginning to think I wasn't going to get any peace.

Then one day she called and said she had to go to the big smoke for a week. Would I be okay? I said I would be fine. She asked me if I would like her to bring anything back for the children. I said, "No, thank you, the children are fine." Then she was gone again.

A few days later, I went to bed early. I was awakened by someone whispering. I turned around and thought I was dreaming. Ten minutes later, the whispering started again. I went into the boys' bedroom, but everything was quiet.

I looked through the window and pulled my head back in fright. I swore I could see a child out there with his face pressed up to the window. I looked again and saw nothing. I grabbed my coat and ran outside. Still nothing.

When I got up the following day, I went to see if there were any footprints around under the window, but there was nothing there. I thought that I must have been dreaming and went back into the house. My days were filled with happiness having the children around. We went exploring the beautiful hillsides.

Then, one day, while we were exploring, Richard said, "We must go this way, Mommy." I asked him why, and he said that Bubo told him. I asked who Bubo was. He smiled and said, "He's my friend." I didn't ask anymore.

We followed him through some bushes. When we got out the other side, it was like a different place. There was a very old house. It was very well kept. The roses were climbing up and over the roof, and the flowers were so beautiful.

I told the boys we could not go any further. It must be somebody's house. But my youngest boy said that Bubo said we have to go to his house. I told him, "Not today." I took his hand and walked back.

We wandered back to the house, and I thought, yes, I would like to do some gardening myself and get the house painted. I thought I would go into town to see if I could get someone to paint it. We jumped into the car and drove twenty minutes to the little village.

There were maybe eight shops there: a greengrocer shop, a chemist, a hardware shop and others. We went into the hardware shop and spoke to the lady there. I asked if they sold paint. She said, "Yes, what colours would I like?"

I asked if she knew anyone who could paint the house. She said, "There is only one person here that could do your house justice. I will tell them tomorrow, and they will be around to see you." I thanked her and looked around. I picked up a shovel, spade fork, and some other tools for pruning.

I was a bit surprised at myself because I had not done much gardening before, but the children thought it was a good idea. We piled the stuff in the car and drove back. It was very peaceful. When the children went to bed, I made myself a cup of tea and stood staring out of the window.

Then, once again, I heard the whispering, and the face came back at the window. It gave me such a fright I dropped my cup. I looked back again, but there was nothing there. I knew I was not dreaming this time or imagining anything.

I lay awake most of the night and decided I would leave the children at home and go down to the village to see what I could find out, but before I knew what was happening, Betsy appeared in my kitchen and said, "Good morning, everyone." Then she looked around and asked, "Where are the children?" I told her it was only half-past six in the morning.

It was too early for the children to get up. She said, "okay", and went and put the kettle on. She looked at me in a strange way and asked if everything was okay. I told her I was thinking about going to town; that strange thing had been happening.

I told her about the little boy who kept whispering at the window. She sat down heavily on the chair and just looked at me. I was not quite sure what to say, so I changed the subject and talked about the house that we found. She looked at me once again and said that it was Maisie's house.

I asked who Maisie was. She said she was a friend and kept on stirring her tea. She said that Maisie had had seven children. The youngest one was Bubo. I asked her what had happened. She said, "I will tell you this evening.

Can you meet me at Maisie's house? Please don't bring your children." I looked at her with surprise. It was the first time I'd heard her talk in a low voice. I said I would be there. She stood up and walked away, and I wondered what had made her so upset.

I put the children to bed and waited for them to fall asleep. It did not take them long as we had been playing out in the woods again, and it always made them tired.

It was a moonlit night, and I was grateful, but I still took my big torch with me. I found the way back to the shrubs and walked through them. Betsy was waiting for me and asked me to come into the house. I was quite surprised that everything was neat and tidy. She put the kettle on as always and asked me to sit down.

She said, "Seven years ago, Maisie's husband Jack had one of his drinking bouts. He used to make moonshine in the hills. He was so crazy with the drink that he killed Maisie and six of the children. He chased Bubo through the forest until Bubo came to the house. But the person that lived there also drank heavily and was asleep, and did not hear Bubo banging on the window for help. That person was me. I have never taken a drop since that day. Bubo's little soul somehow got lost on the way, and he kept calling at the window for help.

I moved into Maisie's house, and I've been here ever since, looking after her flowers and the house for her. I've never forgiven myself for not being there for her." I could not believe what I was hearing.

She showed me some photographs, and I recognised the youngest boy as the one tapping on the window. I said, "I'm so confused. I don't know what to think." Then I remembered a friend of mine told me about a séance.

I asked her if she knew what it was. She said, "I live in the country, but I'm not an idiot." I said, "What about going to the library tomorrow in the village and seeing if we can find some help there?" Betsy agreed.

We walked back through the bushes, and I found my way back to the house. All the time, I thought I could feel someone pulling on my trouser leg. I went to bed that evening thinking of that little boy, the mother, and the other children. The following morning, I awoke to find Betsy holding a cup of tea over my bed. I nearly jumped through the roof.

She smiled and said, "You overslept this morning." I looked at the clock, and it was a quarter past seven. We dropped the two children at the cinema. I thought it would be better if they didn't know what was going on.

We went to the library and asked if we could look through some of the books, and she said, "Yes, what sort are you looking for?" I said, "I'm looking for spiritual books."

She said, "I hope you don't mind me speaking up, but I wondered if it had anything to do with the house that you bought?" I said it was, and she said that no amount of reading would help that family, but she did know of a woman called Meyer who had helped a lot of people in the same circumstances.

She told me where she lived. Betsy said she knew where it was. We jumped into the car and started to climb a huge hill. Betsy said, "I forgot all about her, but I'll be honest, we all thought she was mad." I asked, "Why are we going then?" Betsy said, "We have to try everything." The place looked like an old shack, and Betsy started calling out and clapping her hands. I asked why she clapped.

She said that it was an old custom; when you went on to someone's land, you would clap to let him or her know that you were arriving. I thought what a good idea. Someone came out and started shouting at us to go away, but Betsy was not going to take no for an answer.

She said, "We have come for your help." The old woman said, "You'd better come inside then."She must have had thirty cats. They were all over the place. She told us to sit down, but she had to push the cats off the chair first.

Betsy started to tell her straight away and said that we were worried about Bubo. She said, "Yes, I know, he's been here too." I jumped in and asked, "Why haven't you helped him?" She said, "It's not my place to until he asks for help.

Has he asked for help?"I told her about the boy knocking on the window and whispering. She scratched her head and said, "Okay, I will help. I will come around to your house tonight at 9 o'clock. Be there, both of you."

We stood up and left the house. I said to Betsy, "I hope she knows what she's doing." Betsy replied, "I think she does." We drove back to the little town, stopped, and had a cup of tea at the grocery shop.

The atmosphere was good; everybody wanted to come and talk to us. Betsy looked at her watch and said, "Let's go pick up the children."The children were so excited about the film they shouted over each other, telling us all about it.

I asked Betsy if she would like to stay for tea. She shrugged her shoulders and said, "Why not."Once again, the house was filled with laughter. Betsy was so good with the children. After they were bathed, they went straight to bed. I was hoping that they wouldn't wake up through the night.

Not long after that, I heard a knock on the door, and Meyer came inside. She placed her basket on the table and told us to sit down. She took candles out of the basket and sat them all around the place; at the window, she placed some herbs and put them all around by the candles.

She told us to sit down at the table and wait. She turned the lights off, and we sat in the candlelight. Meyer started to hum some kind of tune, and it was rather nice. She said, "Close your eyes now and try not to move." I grabbed Betsy's hand, and I hung on to it.

The next moment, we could hear whispering and a gentle tap on the window. Meyer shouted, "Come in, come in, I can hear you." The whispering got louder and louder. It was a cry for help that I will never forget.

"Please help my Mommy", he kept crying over and over again. Then Meyer said, "Where is your Mommy, Bubo?" "In the woods", he shouted. She stood up, went outside, and beckoned us to follow her. We walked for twenty minutes or so, and then she stopped. She told us to stay back.

As she went forward, we heard her talking to him, and then it looked like she was holding him in her arms and rocking him.

She started to sing a beautiful lullaby, and after a time, she stood up and came towards us. She said Bubo would rest now, and he would find his mother and his six siblings. We walked back to the house, and Betsy made a cup of tea.

Meyer explained the rest to us. She told us, "When he could not get any help, he went back to find his mother. His father was still lying there drunk. He picked up his father's gun and shot him. Then took the gun and shot himself in the head." I slowly put my cup back on the table and leant back. I thought how much pain that little boy had gone through.

Old Meyer jumped up and said it was time for her to go, and in the same breath, said, "If you want to do anything for the boy, then gather all the children and the mother together in one place with Bubo."When I asked why, she said, "Why not?" That it would be a good thing to do, for other people could then show their respect.

Betsy and I thanked Meyer for helping us. She said it was not for us, and it was for Bubo. Then she was gone. Betsy said that it was the best day's work that she had ever done in her life.

I agreed, saying it was the most unusual thing that I had ever done in my life. We both hugged each other and knew that our friendship would last forever.

6. Nowhere To Run

I felt strange. Scared and frightened, but a peace that I had never known before. I look around me and once again find myself in the memories of Mary Maclair. Here, sitting at the bottom of the huge dam, the water is cold and dark, but I can see the light above me.

My memories went into full swing. I was running away from my father. I could still feel the pain of his belt on my back and legs. I was running, trying to escape from him, stumbling with every blow of the belt. I was getting very weak and found myself crawling on my hands and knees.

Trying so desperately to stand up, another blow, down I went again. I remember thinking, this was it, and then all of a sudden, he was right by my side, cursing and swearing. I could get up, I fought to stand on my feet, and with every ounce of energy I had, I ran until I could not run anymore. I could see the dam now, and I thought if I could only reach it, there would be somewhere for me to hide.

I got closer and closer and started to walk into the water, feeling the coolness on the back of my legs. My whole body was shaking. The water started to heal my aching legs. I went further and further into the water. I did not know how much time it would take for my father to find me again.

At that moment, I felt my body sink to the bottom of the dam. I could see a small light high up in the water. I thought I could hear him shouting my name. I looked up, and I could see him through the water.

It was very difficult to breathe now. I pulled my legs up, wrapped my arms around my knees, and slowly let go of life. I found peace. I could never explain why I felt so safe and secure, and I knew I did not want to leave this place. It was the place I had searched all my life for, a place where no one could ever hurt me again. I found peace within.

7. Till We Meet Again

I slowly let go of her hand as the train was pulling away. I leaned out of the window and shouted, "Till we meet again!" I could still see her in the distance. I sat back in my seat and knew it was love at first sight.

I had just come back from leave, and Mam asked if I could take these few things to the Red Cross shop for her. I replied, "Okay, see you in a moment." I walked down the street to where the little church was, which had a big sign outside saying, "Red Cross".

I walked in and said to the man at the door, "Mother asked me to bring these few things here. Where do I put them?" He smiled and said, "You see that young lady over there; she will take them off you." I looked across, and I thought, what a beautiful girl.

I smiled at her, and she smiled back. I walked over to her and said, "Mother asked me to leave these here." She said, "You must be David." I said, "Yes", and smiled. She put her hand out and said, "My name is Daisy."

At that moment, someone called her, and she walked away. I smiled and went back to the old man at the door. I said, "Pretty girl, isn't she." He said, "Don't get any ideas, young man. That is my Daisy. She is my daughter", and gave me a stern look. I looked back across the hall, and she was waving to me.

I walked down the street to meet a couple of my friends who were on leave with me. Pat, the Irishman, smiled and said, "What have you been up to?" I looked at him with a glint in my eye and said,

"You will never know." We all laughed together as we went in for a pint.

I looked at my watch, and it was six-thirty. I said my farewells and thought, Mother said to be home for six; she is going to have my hide. I thought I'd better take the shortcut. It would be quicker. Just as I turned the corner, I bumped into somebody. It was Daisy. I couldn't believe my luck!

She smiled and said, "Where are you off to in such a great hurry?" I said, "I'm late for tea, and you know what parents are like." She smiled and said, "Yes, I've only got Dad, and he is a handful." We both laughed together.

My first instinct was to stay, but I knew Mother was waiting for me. I nodded and said, "What about tomorrow? The same time, the same place." She said she would with a sparkle in her eyes.

Mam opened the door and said, "David, where have you been?" I said, "Sorry, Mother."I was there the following evening waiting. I waited and thought, she's not going to come. Just as I started to walk away, I heard someone call my name. "David!" I turned around; it was Daisy.

She said she was so sorry, but she could not get away any earlier. I asked her where she wanted to go. She asked, "Could we just walk?" I thought, what a good idea. We went to the canal and sat down on the wall. We seemed to talk for hours. I loved to hear her talk about herself.

She said her mother had died when she was born, and her father and sister had brought her up. She was going to study to be a nurse. As she slowly turned around, I stole a kiss. She looked away with embarrassment.

I said I was sorry and went to hold her hand. She said she did not want to fall in love with someone in the forces. She did not want to be like many of her friends, waiting for their loved ones to come home safely.

I said, "I'm sorry, but sometimes it's better to have loved someone than not loved at all, and if fate throws you a bad one, then you will always have the memories to see you through.

Then, when I'm in Heaven, I can look down and say, 'That was my girl, Daisy.'Hoping my last words would make a difference, she looked even sadder. She stood up and said, "Thank you for the lovely evening."

We walked back together without saying a word. I wanted to hold her hand, but I knew she would not let me, so I said, "I'm only here for four more days, and I must go back." She turned away and walked to her front door.

It was two days later when I saw Daisy again. She looked across at me and waved. I walked towards her and asked if she would like to have tea with Mother and me. She smiled and said, "Yes, what time?" I said six o'clock would be fine. I went home and told Mother. She smiled and said, "Don't worry, David, everything will be fine."

Daisy knocked on the door precisely at six o'clock. We had a lovely tea. Everyone chatted, and Daisy smiled at me, and I thought, yes, I could love this girl forever. She thanked Mother for the lovely evening, and we walked out together.

I asked her if I could walk her home. She said she would be very pleased. On the way, she broke down and cried and said, "I know I did not want to get involved, but I think I'm in love with you. How can that be possible? I have only known you for three days."

I smiled at her, held her in my arms, and said, "I feel the same way." We kissed, and nothing else mattered. We spent the remaining time together, laughing and talking about the future and what we would do together. The next day, she said that she had passed her exams to be a nurse and expected to be going away in the next week or so. I said, "Please come back to me." She said, "I will always be with you, no matter how far apart we are. I promise you." Then she turned around and said, "David, promise you will come back to me."We left it at that.

The following morning, I was due to go back to my squadron. I asked her, "Please do not come to the station. It would be too hard for me to let go of you." She promised me that she wouldn't come. But as the train started to leave the station, Daisy was there waving to me. I was so happy to see her and waved back.

I shouted. "I love you!" I didn't hear any more as the train was so noisy, but I knew she'd told me that she loved me too. During the next months, we were flying planes that were not ready to fly, but we had no choice; it was always "king and country" for us.

Daisy kept sending me letters about what was going on in her life, but I sensed a change in her letters. They were sad. I told her to keep up the good work and that we would be together soon. She told me she was going to see a friend the following day and that they needed her help, but it was really close to the front. In my letter, I wrote back and said, *Please remember I love you. Be careful.* Then, our Squadron Leader said the next flight would be the most important flight of our lives.

That everything was a secret, even to the time that we were leaving the following morning. I remember writing the last words to Daisy. I left the letter on my bed and walked out thinking what a beautiful day. The sun was just coming up, and the sky was the bluest I had ever seen.

Then everything went quickly. We each got into our aeroplanes and took off, and three hours into flying, we heard the sound of firing. I turned around to see where the enemy was. I remember looking at my watch; it was February 15 at quarter to five. Once more, I looked at the sky.

All I could see now was the huge explosion; then nothing. Time had no meaning where I was. I knew I had to do something. I felt myself back on familiar ground. I found myself outside the Red Cross church. I walked in. It was empty. There was a huge pile of newspapers by the door.

One of the papers blew open and turned the pages. I looked down, and it said *Daisy McGuire died in the line of duty on February 15 at quarter to five.* I could not believe what I was reading! I picked up the paper and read again.

As I looked away from the paper, I looked towards the door, and I saw Daisy holding out her hand. She said, "I've come to keep my promise. Shall we go?" I took hold of her hand, and we walked away together.

8. The Window

Here I am, sitting in my chair, and as usual, no one takes any notice. I scream out all the time because that is the only way I can communicate and let people know I am still here. I have been in a wheelchair most of my life. Where did it begin? I don't remember.

My body aches all the time, but no one listens. They think I don't know what's going on because I can't talk. If they only knew. Every day of my life has been the same. Someone gets me out of bed and dumps me in a bath of water.

Sometimes it's nice and warm, but most times it's cold. I can't tell these people. They think it's acceptable to just do what they think is right, and they towel-dry me with no dignity. They dress me with much the same attitude.

I have learnt to blank life out, but I keep on making as much noise as I can because I am afraid if I stop, people will forget I'm alive. Mum called in today as she does every day. She holds me and treats me like a human being, and I know how she yearns for me to put my arms around her and tell her how much I love her.

Mum did not want to leave me here, but she is getting older now, and she is very small and can no longer lift me in and out of the bath or the bed. She stays with me most of the day, and it's funny, but she is like me.

Nobody sees her anymore; she just blends into the background. Like me, she is like clockwork. She comes every day at quarter past ten and leaves at quarter past three. She likes to get home before it gets dark.

She is getting ready to leave now. Oh, how I would like to tell her how much I love her and how much I appreciate her for always being there for me! When my father found out that I was brain-damaged and would never walk, he walked out and never came back.

It's always been mum and me. I sit here and watch her quietly walk away unnoticed. I've wet myself again. I have a nappy on, but it soon gets full up. I will have to wait until someone remembers I'm here and takes me for my evening bath and then bed. It's morning again, and the nurse has not yet come in. I'm glad that one morning out of many is different. I just lay there enjoying the extra time in bed.

A knock comes on my door, and a man walks in. He looks very nice but not very old. I think straight away, will he notice me? He looks at my chart at the end of my bed, smiles and comes towards me. He says, "Did you have a good night's sleep, Tommy?"

I thought I must be dreaming, so I screamed out, making all these strange noises, trying to tell him that, at last, someone was taking notice. He grabs for my hand that I am waving about like a frigging lunatic and smiles at me again, and says, "We will have you out of this bed in ten minutes, washed and ready for breakfast."

I could not believe my ears and, true to his word, I was up, dressed and sitting at the table with other people waiting for my breakfast. I sat patiently waiting; everyone seemed to be talking at the same time. I tried to listen to what was going on. I kept hearing the name James, the new Superintendent.

I wondered if that was the same person that came into my bedroom. Breakfast came and went, and I stayed very quiet. I did not want to miss anything or any conversation.

I felt someone pull my chair out and touch my head. "Did you enjoy your breakfast?" I did not know what to say. It was such a surprise. My arms and legs started to wave around, and I felt like a bloody idiot

. He told me his name was James as he wheeled my chair to the window and said, "I hope you like that view, Tommy."James left me by the window, and for the first time, I got to look out at the world. I prayed nobody would wheel me away.

Everyone used to leave me to look at a wall before, but today was different. I watched people walking around; there was also a dog on the grounds, and people were eating lunch and talking to each other. What a wonderful world, I thought,

please don't shut me off again. James came and got me and touched my head again with a very loving hand. He said, "Are you ready for lunch, Tommy?" I got so excited that my hands and legs started to wave again. I felt like a bloody idiot. James didn't seem to mind. Lunch came and went. I waited and waited, and once again, I felt my chair being turned around, and there was James.

This time, he bent down in front of me and said, "How would you like to go for a stroll with me?" And off we went. My bloody arms went again, waving like an idiot. He turned my chair around, and we both went out into the corridor together. I was so proud of James.

We left the long corridor and went out into the garden. James turned me around and sat on the bench beside me. He said to me, "Have you wondered why your Mother hasn't been here for the last two days?" I thought, bloody hell, I forgot about Mum with all the excitement.

What will she think of me, and where is she? Just at that moment, I had a really bad feeling. I had been so preoccupied with what was going on that I was ashamed to say I had forgotten about Mum. Where is she? I wanted to shout, but only a scream came out. James said, "Your mother has not been very well. She had to go into the hospital, but she's okay." He seemed to know what I was thinking. He said, "Do you want me to take you to see her?" I could not believe what I was hearing. Why had it taken so long for a kind person to understand that although we cannot communicate, we have feelings?

These feelings turn into a hatred of life itself, and you seem to get lost in nothing; you feel nothing, you hear nothing, and you are nothing. Thanks to James, life has just begun.

He asked me, "Would you like to go tomorrow?" It was as though he knew what I was thinking. I was not screaming anymore, and my arms were no longer waving around.

We just sat there together, looking at the flowers and the trees and watching people. I had not known such peace for a long time. Tomorrow, I would see my mother and what else would tomorrow bring?

I have never had tomorrows before; I've always lived for today. James has made me think of the future, and yes, I have had a voice for a short time. Long enough to make people aware that if you see people like me in the streets or in private hospitals, please don't think we are idiots. We are aware of everything around us; we just cannot communicate. It is not such a wonderful place that people like me find themselves living in. It can be a living hell. I'm telling you this story from the other side.

I know a few of you will understand about transforming thoughts from one entity to another. Both entities have to be compatible and understanding. I thank this person for giving me the opportunity to tell my story, which has not yet finished. I am glad to say James took me to see Mother the following day, and she was so pleased to see me.

I did not wave my arms around, only once to try to reach her hand. I need not have worried. James understood what I was trying to say. He told Mum, "Tom has been excited all night and looking forward to seeing you." Mum smiled.

He sat down beside her bed and told her all about our venture into the garden. She looked over and smiled at me. James touched Mum's hand with so much kindness and then told her, "Please don't worry about Tommy. I will always look after him." He did, and Mum passed away two months later. I was so sorry to see her go, and I missed her so much, but James said that life must go on, and it did. Two years later, James got me into a commission house. A house where other people like me stayed, but I am also glad to say so did James.

I lived for another four years after that and passed away on August 31. James will always be with me, and I miss him very much. But I also know while James is there, there's hope for other people like myself. I end this story with the hope that we all have a James somewhere in the future.

God bless them all.

9. My Baby Doesn’t Cry

My baby doesn't cry! I had carried my baby for nine months. The nurse said, “Sorry, but we couldn't save her.” I drifted back into a black sleep, holding onto all that I could.

Then, I slept for two days and two nights. When I woke up, a beautiful light came at me. I could not see. I had to put my hand up to the light to shield my eyes.

Then, from nowhere, I heard a voice saying, “You must go back.” It came again, “You must go back.” “No”, I said, “Please don't send me back.” I began to feel a beautiful feeling of warmth and love. It was calling me further and further in, into where I don't know.

But the feeling of love was incredible. I didn't want to let go, and then, just as quickly, it left. I was back. Feelings were coming back again. Then darkness came, and I heard a voice calling, "Mary. Mary wakes up." My eyes flew open.

I found myself in the hospital. I looked around, and it looked very sterile. "I am sorry", the nurse said. I asked, "What for?" She said, "Nothing", and smiled. I asked, "What am I doing here?" I will tell the Doctor you are awake", the nurse said.

She smiled and left. I lay there for a while. Then, a doctor came in, looked at me, and said, "How are you feeling today?" I said, "Fine, thank you." He never said any more. He just walked away.

Then someone knocked on my door and asked, "May I come in?" The lady told me her name was Wendy. She pulled a chair up and sat by my bed. "Do you remember what happened?" I said, "No." She said, "Loss comes in many ways." I looked alarmed and asked, "What loss?" I leaned back into my pillow and felt nothing.

I listened to what she was saying, but nothing seemed to sink in. What baby? Whose baby? She left then without a word. I had been there for about four days, and strangely, I did not have visitors. Not that I had a family of my own.

Then, late in the afternoon, Dr Barite came and said, "We are moving you to another hospital where you can be properly looked after." Where am I going?" I asked.

The next moment, a man came in with a wheelchair and asked me to get in. Funny, you don't ask questions. So I just got in. Outside, an ambulance was waiting, and we quickly drove off.

On arriving, the nurse quickly got me into bed. Not long after that, the Doctor arrived. He told me his name was Gerard and started to explain what had happened to me. I said, "No, not me. I've never been pregnant."The Doctor patted my hand and walked away.

Lunch came and went. I still could not understand. I slowly fell back to sleep. I felt myself drifting once again. This time, it was different. I was falling deeper and deeper down and further still. A feeling of emptiness and loneliness came over me. I heard myself crying and calling, "My baby doesn't cry! Oh, God!" I could hear myself screaming and screaming. Someone came in and held me.

I took a deep breath, and reality stepped in. Memories came flooding back. The baby, yes, I remember now. At that moment, the sun came rushing in, and a new day began.

10. Left But Not Forgotten

I felt sad and oh so scared. I felt loneliness all around me. I saw a slide, and the swings started to come into my vision, and I heard a child crying. It seemed so far away. I listened for a while, and then I saw a child, a boy, in blue jeans and a red t-shirt with a yellow pattern. His hat was back to front.

I called him, but he did not hear me, so I sang a song. "Humpty Dumpty sat on the wall." Then I sang, "Baa Baa Black Sheep". He stopped crying and started to listen. I got closer and closer, singing nursery rhymes. I got as close as I could without scaring him. Then I whistled like a bird.

He said to me, "Do you know where my mummy is? Because I think I'm lost." I sat as close to him as I could."I think I saw your mummy over there."

Where?" He asked."Just over there. Can you see her?" He said no. I told him to sing his favourite song, the Little Mermaid, and she would hear him and come to him.

He started to sing, and I got closer. He gently put his hand in mine and said, "Please don't let him hurt me again. I want to see my mummy."I said, "I promise", and the little boy said, "The man took me in his car, hurt me, and left me here. I called and called, but nobody came.

It was dark, so I knew mummy would not be able to find me." I held his hand very softly, not tight. I said, "Your mummy found you, darling, I'm here."And when he looked up, he saw his mummy's face, not mine.

He felt his mummy's arms around him and his mummy's kisses. And in that moment of happiness, a great light came, and he was in someone else's arms. It was someone of great importance, someone who loved him very much. I smiled and walked away.

11. The Crossing

We hid in the old barn until someone called us. It was very dark at that moment. There were seventeen people with me. Most of them were young children. The year was 1817, and it was February 22. We were all huddled together, waiting for someone to tell us if it was safe to come across.

Just at that moment, someone called. We had to cross a small bridge to reach where he was calling us. We scrambled down the hill and found this person waiting. He looked to be in his forties. He kept shoving us forward.

We were very close to the sea now. I could smell the salt air. All of a sudden, he pushed us all to the floor. "Shush", he said. After a few minutes of being too scared to breathe, he said we should be safe now.

We have pushed forward again. One of the children started to cry, and he pushed us even faster. We were aware of a small bright light coming towards us, and the next moment, we were loaded into a small boat and slowly left the shore behind. It seemed only a few moments before we were quickly loaded on to a big boat. We were then pushed down underneath the deck.

Its pitch black down there. We were told someone would give us light in a moment. We move off into the open seas very quickly. Twenty minutes went by, and we were still waiting. I looked up, and all I could see was some kind of a grid. I called out, "We need a light down here."

A few moments later, someone threw a candle down between the bars and one match. I quickly lit the candle and looked around. It was so dismal down there, and the smell was so bad. We started to spread out and look for anywhere that we could sit or lie.

I managed to find some old sacks and wrap them around the children. We were all hungry and thirsty. It is funny that we never thought of hunger whilst we were trying to escape. Now, the hunger pains were strong. "Please place all your food in this cloth so it can be shared equally", I asked them all. I looked down after a few moments, but there was very little food. I decided to be brave again and called up, "We need food and water down here, please."There was no answer.

I called again and again, but there was still no answer. Then, when I had given up hope, someone put their hand through the grid and dropped a lump of bread which dropped beside me.

The next moment, water was handed down in a cup. I was told to quickly return the cup. I went around and gave people a small drink and then handed the cup back. Someone said, "Did you get a drink?" I said, "No." He said, "Next time." We were all feeling very sick now with very little water to drink. Unable to wash, we all started to smell quite strong.

I felt very sorry for the children. One little boy came to me and said, "I'm hungry." I sat him on my knee and gently rocked him. I started to sing and then noticed the other people were joining in. I suppose it was lifting their spirits up.

I don't know how long we were down there, but I think it was around three days. The person kept bringing a small quantity of bread and water and told me they were having difficulty landing because of us being on board. Later that morning, we heard a lot of shouting and confusion, and the old boat seemed to be picking up speed. Then, we heard a big bang.

Then, it started to sway to one side. We all started to scream. Everything happened so fast; the water started to come in through the grid. The boat was on its side, and we were screaming for help. We couldn't loosen the grid.

Then, from nowhere, a pair of arms came down and grabbed me, pulling me up. I quickly turned around, and the water was filling up now. I saw people starting to flow out through the top of the grate. I pulled up as many as I could, and the next thing I knew, the boat turned completely upside down, and we were back in the water again.

I felt myself sinking. I tried so desperately to swim to the top, but my clothes were too heavy; they weighed me down. I went down until there was nowhere else to go but to the bottom. I could feel myself sitting there. No longer gagging for air, I slowly watched the other people sinking down all around me. I stood up. I walked to where I saw little baby Clare and put my arms out to catch her. I knew she was dead. I cradled her in my arms and went to look for little Bobby. He lay there so still. My heart broke.

I walked over to where the woman, whose baby I still held, lay face down. I stood there looking around, which seemed like hours, but I believe it was only moments. Then, I felt the courage to stand up and call these people to follow me.

For those who were still lying or sitting down, I gently tapped on the shoulder and said, "It's time to go." I watched them in amazement. The baby's mother stood up and gently took the baby from me and cradled her in her arms.

The other woman stood up and went to look for her son, then gently lifted him up to stand by her side. When everyone was standing, I looked around and started to walk to what seemed like a door that was opening.

The closer we got, the bigger the door became. I stopped and thought for a moment. Will anyone remember the Edinburgh boat that was sunk with all hands on board? What would my family say? They had saved all their money to give me a better life away from the fighting and killing that was taking place in Ireland.

Was this to be the last of me, I wondered. As I saw the last one through, I thought of all the other people who had died in the name of religion. I went quickly through the door, not leaving behind anything but taking all the memories of the past and with hopes for a new future.

12. An Empty Chair

Every day, I walk past and touch your chair. I stand there looking out of the window; the wind is coming in strong now. I can look out as far as the eye can see. I watch the beautiful trees that you planted waving about, telling me that everything is going to be okay.

You promised me that we would live on this land together forevermore. Where are you now? I close my eyes, and you are here with me. I open them, and you are gone.

I hear your whisper in the rustle of the trees. I hear your call in the wind that whistles through the door. When I lay in my bed at night, I can still feel your arms around me. I smell your hair and listen to you telling me how much you love me.

When I wake up in the morning, there is still an empty chair. It's been three months since I last saw you. I watched you walk away, smile and tell me, as you have many times before, "I will see you when the sun rises." But the sun never rises anymore. I waited for you to come home, but you never came. I stood at the window looking for you. I sat on the porch waiting for you. You never came.

I look around an empty room and see an empty chair.

It was a couple of days before Christmas, and things were tough. You told me you were going to look for more work and that you would be back soon. You never came back.

The sun is just coming up, and I remember the times we used to sit together and watch the sunrise. You used to say that this land is the greatest gift, and one day it will be ours. You spent every hour you had cleaned the land for planting.

Every day, it was a struggle just to buy the seeds, and every day, you came home just a little bit more tired. It took us both a full year to just tidy up the front. I watched you planting trees so there would be shade in the summertime. We had a vegetable patch, and every day, you would go out and pick some.

Nothing seemed too much trouble. I used to watch you from the kitchen window and think how blessed I was when I heard a car coming in the distance. I hoped it was the Sheriff with the news. I watched him get out of his car; he didn't look very happy. He shook the dust from his shirt, waved to me, and asked, "Can I come in?"

I told him I had a cold drink for him, and without taking a breath, I asked him if he had any news. "I'm sorry", he said, "we have found nothing. We spoke to Mr Dowling; he was the last one to see your husband. He said everything was well and that he was just going to the store to pick up some beans, and nobody saw him after that. It's a mystery.

There are only 3,000 people in the township. How can you lose one man?" I sat down, clutching the tea towel. He said, "How long has it been now?"' I said a little over three months. He said they would still keep looking, but he could not understand what happened.

I walked behind him as he left and waved goodbye to him. I walked into the kitchen, and there was an empty chair. I shouted out, "Where are you, my darling? Tell me where you are!" At that moment, the door closed shut. I thought, it's the wind and looked away. I had not been eating very well, so the veggies were going to seed.

But I needed to water them. I thought about how he would be upset if I let them die. I went out and sprinkled water on them and walked back to the house. I looked at the chair again, and I think it's moved. I must have knocked it when I went by.

So I went to the chair and straightened it back into its position. I slowly walked to the bedroom. I lay on the bed and called his name. I heard a tap on the door. I jumped up quickly because I didn't get visitors. Who would be knocking on my door? There was no-one there.

I closed the door, walked to the chair, straightened the cushion up, and walked back towards the bedroom. I heard a scraping noise and immediately turned around. There was no-one there. I stood there for a moment and looked around. Something was wrong with the chair. It had been moved.

I walked towards the chair, put it back in its position again, and looked around. For the first time, I looked at the chair and found myself sitting in it. I leaned back and placed my head the way he used to place his. I put my arms and hands on the arms of the chair the way he placed his. I leaned back and let my mind wander; it felt comfortable.

In no time at all, I had fallen asleep. I saw my husband again, smiling at me and waving, just like the last time I remembered him. I watched him drive away until I could no longer see the truck, only a dust cloud. Then I thought I heard him call my name.

I woke up and went to the door. The night was coming in fast now. I knew there would be no-one there. I slowly turned around and went to light the kero lamp. I took some bread and a little cold meat and made a sandwich. I boiled the kettle and sat there quietly, eating the sandwich.

There was no noise; the wind had died down. The trees stopped their rustling, and it was just stillness. I was so lonely.

I dropped the sandwich onto the floor and cried until I had no more tears left. As I looked up, I saw the chair move again. I thought I was seeing things.

I looked around, but there was nothing that could move the chair. For one moment, I was scared, and then I remembered one day at the library, some of the girls were talking about death and that sometimes spirits come back.

I thought, could it be my husband? I called his name and stood behind the chair, but nothing happened. I laughed at myself and said what a stupid person I was. I went to bed. The following day, I got up, but the day was different.

I wanted to move the chair to the front veranda and just sit there. So that was what I did. I sat there for a couple of hours, just looking out and remembering how I'd watched my husband work the fields.

Once again, I must have dropped off to sleep because I could hear him calling my name. But this time, it was different. This time, I was still asleep, and it felt like I was down a big hole. I called, 'Where are you, my love?"Then I woke up, and I sat there for a moment and remembered what my husband was holding in his hand. It was a bit of timber with some writing on it. I tried so desperately but could not remember.

I slowly got up from the chair, made myself a cup of tea, and thought, what is my husband trying to tell me? I went back to his chair and talked to him. I just had this feeling that he was trying to tell me something, but I could not sleep or think of him anymore that day.

I was so cross with myself for not remembering one small thought. I went to bed early that night. This time, I heard him calling me again in my sleep. He was taking me back to the first time we saw this beautiful land together.

I remember him telling me that this was his father's land and about the dreams they both had of clearing the land together. He would tell me the story about the old watering hole and how he loved the land. I lay there remembering, and then all of a sudden, the timber was there in front of me.

The old mine shaft! I jumped up, grabbed my coat, and ran through the door straight to the old truck. Could I drive it? Yes, I could. I jumped in without hesitation and turned on the key. But it would not start.

Then I remembered my husband telling me, "Don't panic, stop everything, turn the key on slowly." That's what I did, and the engine started. I put the clutch in, and off I went. I was getting quite sick from the vibrations of the clutch as I had not learned to use it properly.

I recognised the hill and drove straight for it, and when I got to the path, I stopped the engine and got out. There was the broken sign that I had seen in my husband's hands. I quickly went to the front of the tunnel, but I could not see anything.

I thought I'd better go get the Sheriff and see if he could help me. I jumped back in the truck and drove away. When I got to the Sheriff's office, I told him what had happened. He smiled at me and said, "You've been listening to too many old wife's tales."I said, "Please, give it a try. That's all I ask."

He looked at me, smiled, and said, "Okay, I haven't got anything to do this afternoon. But on one condition: we go in my car." I nodded and quickly jumped in, and we were off down the road in minutes.

When we got to the mineshaft, he said he did not think anyone had been there for years but started to look around. Then he bent down and picked something up. He said, "This is your husband's rifle. Why would he leave it here?" I said, "He never goes anywhere without it." He walked towards the old well and looked down. He told me to stay back, not to come.

I panicked and ran over to him. He said, "Go back."He said he did not understand how he fell into the well, but I knew what he was saying. He told me to get into the car. Minutes later, we drove off back to town.

He got a few men together, and they went back to pick up my husband's body. I waited there with a few of the ladies until they returned. I heard one of the men saying that he had been clutching a piece of timber when he fell into the well.

My husband had been trying to get the old well working when he accidentally fell in. The Sheriff asked me how I knew about the old mine. I told him my husband took me there a long time ago.

He said, "How did you know about the timber he held in his hand?" I told him my husband came to me while I slept. He just looked at me with a certain look and walked away.

I've learned not to miss him so much because, now and again, the chair does move, the door does bang, and someone knocks gently on the door. I know my husband is still with me. And we will live on this land together forever more.

13. Where Is He Now?

I look at the clock; it is five minutes to five. I put the knife down. I was trying to prepare the tea, but once again, I'd run out of time. He will be fine; he will talk to his friends and their mothers until I get there. I pull up at the school, and he is sitting there waiting for me.

He jumps into the car and gives me his special smile, "Hi there, Mum." I reply, "How are things?" "Great", he says, "just great." We pull up, and he rushes indoors. "Mum, look what I made for you today."

It was a picture of him and me in a beautiful garden together. He said, "The lady showed me how to draw this, Mummy, isn't it beautiful?' I smiled, took his drawing from him, and asked, "Where do you want me to put this one, Bobbi-Lee?"

His name is Robert, but I call him Bobbi-Lee. He said, "Can we find a special place for this one, Mummy?" I thought for a moment and said, "Right in front of the living room door." He smiled at me and said, "I knew you would find a special place, Mummy."Bobbi-Lee was coming up to seven years old, but he was old for his age and very considerate to everyone.

I told him that his Nanny would be here soon. He told me not to tell her about his picture; see if she could find it. The three of us had a wonderful evening together. Mother was getting tired now, so I told her to get ready and that I would take her back home. But as usual, she said the bus would do her fine.

The following day, I dropped Bobbi-Lee off at school and went on to work. Just as I was taking lunch, one of the ladies from the other departments came and said, "There is a phone call for you. You can take it in my office." I smiled and said, "Thank you", and walked behind her

I picked up the phone, and it was Bobbi-Lee's school. The nurse said, "I'm sorry to bother you, but could you please come to the school? Bobbi has hurt himself quite badly." I dropped everything straight away and told my boss I must go. I went through the doors out to my car.

When I arrived at the school, the nurse said, "I had to send him to hospital. We could not stop the bleeding." I did not stop to ask what had happened; I just jumped back in the car and went straight to the hospital.

I asked at the front desk, "Can I see Bobbi-Lee?" The young nurse said, "He's in the other room. Would you like to go in?"I followed her in, and Bobbi-Lee held out his hands to me and said,

"Mummy, I was scared without you." I told him everything was going to be okay.

The doctor came in just then and asked me to step outside. He said that he had concerns about what was causing Bobbi-Lee's bleeding. I asked why that was. He said that he had taken it upon himself to do a blood test. He said that the results came straight back.

He said, "Could you come into my office?" I looked at Bobbi-Lee and said, "I won't be long, darling."The doctor did not mince his words. He said, "We would like to keep your son in for some more tests." I asked what tests those would be. He said, "Bobbi-Lee hit his head. We had a problem stopping the bleeding. Since then, we have found a growth just behind Bobbi's ear lobe. We want to do some more tests and see what it is."I asked, "Can I stay with him?" He said, "Of course." I went back to Bobbi-Lee's room and said, "We are going to stay in this nice place tonight. Shall we do some drawing together?" He said, "Why can't we go home, Mummy?"

I told him that the doctor would like to see him again. He looked at me and smiled.

The night quickly passed, and the following morning, the nurse came and took some more blood for tests on Bobbi-Lee. It was later on in the morning that the doctor came and asked if I could come to his office. I put down the book, waved to Bobbi-Lee, and said I would not belong.

When I got to the doctor's office, he said, "I'm sorry. We have found a small brain tumour." I gasped with disbelief. He said he would like to operate the following morning. He said, "If we get it at the right time, Bobbi-Lee will be fine." I asked, "If not, what then?" He said who knows. He said he was sorry he couldn't give me better results and hoped I would act quickly for Bobby's sake.

The quicker the operation was done, the better for Bobbi Lee. I could not believe what I was hearing. The nurse came and said, "Let's go outside for a moment and have a cup of tea." I don't know why, but I asked for coffee instead.

She sat me down outside and, not long after, came to join me. She was such a nice nurse. Her name was Margaret. She started to explain to me what was going to happen, but my mind still would not accept what she was saying.

She gently touched my hand and said, "If you need me, please ask the Matron on duty, and she will come and get me."She also said, "It doesn't matter about the time. If I'm not at the hospital, this is my home number", as she scribbled some numbers down and passed them to me. She said, "I must go on now", and swiftly walked away.

I sat there for a while, trying to take everything in, and then a flash of Bobbi-Lee came into my mind, and I quickly jumped up and went back to him.

In the ward was another little boy, and they were playing together. Bobbi-Lee said, "Look, Mummy, he's got a big bandage on his head. Doesn't he look funny?" I don't think he realised what he was saying, but the other little boy didn't seem to mind at all.

The nurse came back in and said, "I'm sorry, but the doctor needs a decision today." Without thinking, I said yes. I know that if I had taken any more time, I would have said no, and that would not have been in his best interest.

The doctor said after the operation that everything went fine, but he could not promise that it would not come back again. But for now, we had a life to look forward to. The doctor said Bobbi-Lee could go home in a week's time.

It was six months later when Bobbi-Lee complained of headaches. I panicked and phoned the nurse straight away. Margaret came straight to the phone. I told her that Bobbi-Lee was having headaches. She said she would make an appointment for him to come tomorrow morning for X-rays.

The following morning, we were back at the hospital, and the doctor said, "I'm sorry, but the tumour came back." I closed my eyes and tried to shut out his words. Bobbi-Lee was once more admitted to the hospital, and more tests were done, but after a month, I took Bobbi-Lee home.

Things were not getting any better. We spent a lot of time drawing pictures together. Then, one day,

Bobbi-Lee said, "Will you sit on my bed with me, Mummy?" I said, "Yes, darling." I lay beside my son and held him in my arms. The last words my son said to me were, "I love you, Mummy."

As I heard him take his last breath, tears were running down my cheeks. While I held my son in my arms, I told him about the beautiful life that we had together and why I would always love him. I told him what a brave little boy he was and how proud I was. I don't know how long I lay there. Then I heard my mother come in the back door.

She just looked at me and knew that it was all over. She put her bag down and cried. The next few weeks were terrible. Some days, I was there, and some days not. I found myself spending a lot of time by Bobbi-Lee's graveside. Mother said that she was worried about me, that I was losing too much weight.

Week after week, I would lay there on the grass by Bobby's grave. Then, one day, my heart broke with sobs coming from the bottom of my soul, and I cried out to my son, "Where are you now?"The next moment, I felt someone take hold of my hand, and my son was there.

He was saying, "Come, Mummy, and meet all my friends and Grandpa." I felt myself standing up and walking with my son's hand in hand. Everything seemed to be so bright. He took me to the garden that I remember so well.

All through Bobbi-Lee's illness, he would draw the same garden with the most beautiful flowers and a beautiful lady standing there with white wings. As we got closer, Bobbi-Lee stopped and said, "The lady wants to talk to you, Mummy."

I looked up, and she said, "Everything is going to be okay. Bobbi-Lee is well and happy. He was not resting here very well, so we thought it would be a good idea to show you that he was okay."

I saw a most beautiful smile come to the lady's face as she looked towards Bobbi-Lee. My son looked up at me and said, "I'm okay, Mummy, I'm okay." As he let go of my hand, I watched him walk towards the beautiful angel, and at that moment, my heartache was released.

I turned around and saw a new world opening up. I shouted out, "Bobbi-Lee is fine! Bobbi-Lee is happy!" As I walked back home, I had to walk past my mother's house. I knocked on her door and said, "Put the kettle on, Mother. I'm home."

14. Please Answer Me

I'm calling, "Where are you?" As I sit back on the ground, I shake my head, trying to make some sense of what's happening. But there is a strange sense of emptiness around me. I look down at my hands. Everything seems to be okay, so why do I feel like I do?

Once more, I shake my head, trying so desperately to remember. To remember what? I ask myself. But nothing comes. I look around, and there's nothing but emptiness. I don't know what to do. My head hurts so much.

I remember hearing a loud bang, and everything went black. "What was that?" I ask again, "What bang?" I touch my head, and it still hurts. Then I remember someone calling my name. Is it my name? I am so confused. Then nothing.

Again, I lie back and once more try to find out what has happened. Again nothing. Then I heard a strange noise. Was it someone calling me? I feel that someone knows me, but I don't recall the name. I feel this person coming closer to me. I couldn't see anything, and then someone said to me, "Brian, let go." I think, what does she want me to let go of? I look at my hands, but there's nothing there.

The voice says again, "Let go of your soul, Brian."I'm so confused. I can't seem to clear my head. What does the voice mean, let go of my soul? Once more, I shake my head, trying to make sense of what is happening.

Then I heard the sweetest voice saying, "I will always love him." As I reach out, a picture comes into my mind, and I see a beautiful lady standing there by a graveside with two small children. The young lady is holding their hands.

Someone tries to take her away, but she wants to stay. The other person says, "It's for the children's sake, Mary. Please, we must go." Her cries are breaking my heart.

Who is this lady that my heart so deeply cries out for? Then, in the next minute, I heard the voice again, "You must let go, Brian." I close my eyes and shut the voice out. I feel myself drifting back to where the young lady is and watching her climb into the car with the children. My mind follows them until they come to a house. Then, for one quick moment, I think I recognise something, but I don't know.

I can't believe how sad this person is. I follow her into the house, and I look around the room. It feels strange; it feels as though I belong here. I look around, and I see photos of people on the walls, and just as I'm passing a mirror, I see a reflection. I look at the pictures on the wall and see the same person looking back.

I don't quite understand what is going on. I turn around and walk into the other room. I hear people talking and saying how sorry they all are. I stand by the side of the young lady. I know her name is Mary, and I feel this beautiful connection with her. I gently put my hand on her shoulder, but strangely, I could not feel anything.

I pulled my hand away quickly and thought, that felt strange.

One of the children comes running in and walks straight past me without seeing me. Things are getting more complicated. Who am I, and what have these people got to do with me? I wander into another room that looks like a bedroom. I see photos there on the side table. We were married. There in front of me was a photo. Mary was in a beautiful white wedding gown.

I staggered back and thought, what is happening? I fall over a chair, but the chair doesn't move. I quickly get up and go to the door, but the door doesn't open; then I'm through. I'm thinking once more that something's wrong. I fall down the stairs. I sit there, trying to pull myself together.

I look up, asking, "What's going on? Please tell me." The next moment, the person calls again, "Let go, Brian." I shout in anger, "Let go of what?" All of a sudden, the light seemed to go straight through me, and I fell back. As I lay there, I could see Mary and me laughing.

Mary says she won't be long, she's just going shopping. "Don't stay in the workshop too long", she calls. I answer, "No, darling." I put my hands in my pocket and went to the back of the house where I had the workshop. When I look through the window, I see a huge desk.

I'm starting to remember. I was some kind of draftsman. I pick up a large ruler. I look down and see a huge business complex, and my memories come flooding back.

I sit back in the chair and just look around. Then, all of a sudden, I hear someone running up the path. I think it's one of the children and I smile to myself. Then, someone comes into the workshop and shouts, "Give me some money!" And again, "Give me some money!"

I look around, and there's a person in front of me. He is waving a gun. I don't think he knows what he's doing. He's looking under my paperwork for something. I'm shouting all the time, "There's no money in here!" I go to stand up, and the gun is pointed at my head. I remember the last look on his face.

Now I remember the photos of my beautiful Mary. I remember the children, and I remember all that once was. As I stand up and look around, nothing seems to have changed except the date, the twelfth day of August. That was the last day that I'd written in my book, but as I look at the calendar, that date is six months later. What has happened to me at that time? And what did I do? I will not leave this place until my questions have been answered.

I call out, "If you want me to let it go, then I suggest you fill in the gaps because I'm not going anywhere."

Nobody answers me, and nothing changes around me, so I decided to stay until someone answers my questions. I sit back in my chair and wait.

Then I hear a little girl's voice, and I see her coming towards me. She asks, do I mind if she sits by me? I reply, "No." She says, "Do you want to know what happened?"' I say "Yes", and then I think, how would the little girl know what had happened to me?

She replies, "I know everything about you, Brian." I immediately realise she knows what I'm thinking. She smiles at me, and my heart melts. I say, "Okay." She told me I must try to understand. Everyone crosses over differently. I ask, "What's this crossing over?" She says, "It's like going from one place to another place, but in thought only."

I say, "How can you go from one place to another in thought only." She smiles, then laughs and says, "How else would you travel when you've left your body behind?" And laughs again.

Then I realised what she was saying. That I'm dead. Then I asked her, "In that case, why can't I see myself as I was?" She answered that things got a bit confusing with the injury I had to my head. "What was in your mind before the accident? Do you remember?"

It was all slowly making sense now, but I had a lot more questions to ask her. "Why did it take so long?" "How long?" she asks. "Six months", I say. "Six months", she replies, "is the time on the Earth plane, but in our time, it was only a few moments." I try to understand what she is saying, but I am still very confused.

She says to me, "I will try and explain. If I asked you to run across the field now, how would you do it?" I say, "I don't know." She tells me to close my eyes and see myself on the other side of the field. I closed my eyes and went to open them to tell her something, and I was on the other side of the field. She smiles and says, "Simple, isn't it? How long would it have taken you when you were alive?"I say, "About ten minutes." Once again, she laughs.

She says, "Your body is only in your mind. You will understand soon." She sits there on my desk, swinging her little legs and smiling so cheekily at me. I laugh.

I ask, "Does this happen to everyone?" She says, "I told you at the beginning that everyone has a different path to take when they die. Yours was a broken one.

The understanding was too confusing for you, so you held on to the last memory and the memories of life."Then I ask, "Where am I?" She says, "Not quite there."

I say, "How do I get to the other side, and when will I get there?" She replies, "All of these questions are up to you." I ask, "What happens when I get to the other place? What happens if I don't like it?" She smiles and says, "You can always come back."

I stop and think for a moment. Then I ask, "What is going to happen to my wife and two children?'" She looks at me and says, "They will be fine. They also will travel on their journey one day, but in the meantime, they will be fine."

I ask, "How do I know you are telling me the truth?" She replies with a smile, "Because I am you." Now, it was getting even more confusing. She says, "You are me, I am you; we are one of the same. We have been, and we always will be. I am the side of you that will help you to conclude your journey. Things will be fine when you are ready.

Just think of me, and I will be here." I say, "Not just yet." She says she understands. I say, "What if I change my mind?"

She looks at me and says, "You won't." I watch her walk away, and it's a funny thing to say, but I really do see myself walking away.

15. The Post Box

The war is nearly over. I walk by the same postbox every day. Should I post these letters? I can't bring myself to, but what is the alternative?

A stranger walks by and says good morning. He looked so much like my Tommy that I turned around and looked in the direction he was going, and my feet automatically followed him.

He stops and smiles at a young lady in a coffee shop and sits down by her side. I quickly walked up to the counter and asked, "Can I have a cup of tea, please?" The waiter says, "If you would like to sit down, Madam, I will bring your tea to you."

I was careful not to let the young man see me again, so I sat at the back of the shop. It did not take long, and the tea was placed in front of me. I could not stop my memories from going back to my

Tommy. It was around the same time in May that I first met him.

I was strolling along the street with my younger brother when a soldier passed by and said, "Good morning." I looked up and said good morning back.

He smiled with such a beautiful smile; I fell in love at that moment. But he just kept on walking. I thought of him all day and all night. The next day, I took my brother for a walk, but he was not there when we passed him at the fruit shop yesterday. Then Mr Denny called out, "Could you please take these potatoes to Mr Stevens down the road as he can't get out today." I shrugged my shoulders and said yes.

I knocked on Mr. Stevens's door, and what a surprise! The young man opened the door. It must have been a shock because he laughed out loud and said, "We meet again, young Missy. And what can

I do for you?" I told him that Mr Denny had asked me to bring these potatoes.

He smiled at me and called out, "Dad, someone here to see you", and asked me and my brother to come in. The old man was sitting in a chair. He smiled at me and asked me to come closer.

He took my hand and thanked me for the potatoes. He said to Tommy, "Would you be so kind as to make young Missy a cup of tea." I said, "No, thank you. I must be getting home."

The young man smiled at me and said, "Dad, remember this little Missy because she will be my wife one day." I was so embarrassed, and I ran through the door and into the street.

My little brother asked, "Terri, are you really going to marry him?" I smiled to myself and thought, yes, one day, maybe, as we skipped along the pavement back to where we lived.

I did not see Tommy again for a couple of months. Once again, I had to go to the fruit shop, and there he was all smiles. "I've been looking for you, Missy." I said, "My name is not Missy; it's Terri." He gave me that special smile.

"How would you like to walk to the park with me?"

"I don't know", I replied. Once again, he gave me that special smile and took my hand, and we walked together to the park. We sat on a bench closest to the pond where we could watch the ducks.

He told me his name was Tommy and that he had been in the army for three years now. I told him everyone was saying the war was coming to an end. He said, "I hope so. I hate it over there. Most of my friends have died, and I don't want to be one of them." I asked him, "When will you be going back?" He said in two or three days, then smiled and held my hand.

He asked, "Would I like to go to the pictures?" but I said I would have to ask Mum first. He smiled again and said, "Let's do it now." We walked back to where I lived. It was a nice house, but we had to share it with two other families. Dad was also in the army.

Mum took in lodgers to help with the running of the house, and we needed the money. Tommy opened the door for me, and I called, "Mum!" She was a little upset at first, but I reminded her I was now eighteen.

She smiled at me and stroked my hair, then looked at Thomas and said, "You look after my daughter (mind)."

He said, "Yes, Ma'am." After that, we were inseparable, and before he left, he asked me to wait for him. We would be married when he returned. I said, "Yes, with all my heart."

It was only three months later that I was asked to go and see Tommy's father. He was waiting for me when I arrived. The door was opened, and he called me in and asked me to sit down.

He said that Tommy was missing in action and had not yet been found. I asked how that could be. He said he was not sure of the situation, that he had received a letter this morning, and promised me he would let me know if things changed. I thanked him and walked away.

I never heard anything, but in the meantime, I got really sick, and Mum had to take me to the doctor. I had been sick a few years before, but not like this. I could not keep anything down. I had really bad headaches, and I also was losing a lot of weight. I had been so ill that the doctor said I must go to the hospital straight away.

They examined me and did some tests, which took two days, and then I asked my mother to come back in. We both sat there holding each other's hands, and the doctor said, "You have leukaemia." My mother burst out crying.

I asked what it was, and the doctor explained. He told us there would be a lot of pain and anguish in the end and that he could not promise a long life. Mother asked, "How long has she got?" The doctor looked at me with sad eyes and said, "Maybe six months to a year."

I could not believe what I was hearing. We walked slowly home together. People spoke to us in the streets, but we did not hear anything. My heart was beating so fast. Was this really true? Was I dreaming? No, I looked at my mother's face, and I knew.

I sat down that evening to tell Tommy in a letter, but I could not find the words. I seemed to drift into sickness more quickly, and then, one day, a message came for me to go and speak with Tommy's father. I was afraid that he would know I was ill. I had gotten so thin that people didn't recognise me. So I decided to write a letter to him. I wrote a letter to his father and one to my Tommy. "I'm so sorry, but I broke my promise. I could not wait for you. I have married someone else."

The tears slid down onto the paper. I just could not face Tommy and let his father see me so sick. And what of the future? There would be no future for Tommy and me, so it was kinder for it to finish this way.

I told Mum about the letters. She held me in her arms and said, "Yes dear, I believe it's for the best", and asked if I would like her to post them.

I said no and walked out. I carefully put the letters into the post box and walked away.

I heard that Tommy was home. I heard he had been sick for a long time, too. I kept myself to myself and never went out. It was two months later when the doorbell rang, and Mum's friend went to answer it. She called, "Someone to see you, Terri." I did not answer.

I did not feel like seeing anyone. Then I heard a gentle knock on the door, and Tommy was already peeping his head around it.

I could not believe my eyes. He started to walk towards me, and I noticed that he had lost a leg. He asked if he could sit down, and I said yes. He told me when he got my letter that he, too, did not want me to see him like this.

Then his father said, isn't it better to be half a man, than no man at all? "I'd heard that you were sick. At the time thought it would be better all-round for both of us but I could not forget you. I thought it better to have you for a short time than not have you at all."

In the next moment, I was in his arms, and I thought, yes, I could live with this memory for the rest of my life.

16. Waiting By The Graveside

I found myself waiting by the graveside. I don't know how long I was there; I just knew something was different. I looked over to the headstone. I saw my mother and father's names there. I could not remember anything. I tried so hard to remember what I was doing here, and just one thought came to me: the hospital. I looked around, and I could see a tall building. I was drawn to it, and I slowly walked towards it.

It felt strange that no one spoke to me; when I asked questions, nobody answered. I walked into the lift. There were other people with me. I let them press the buttons. One pressed number one, and one pressed number three, and I thought, I hope someone pressed number four, but nobody did. I don't know why, but I sensed that I could not press the buttons, so I just waited. Then, a man and his daughter walked in, and the daughter pressed number four.

Then up we went. I let them get out at first and looked around to see where I was. It did not look like a hospital. It was one long corridor. I started to walk. I looked through some of the windows, but there were no people in there. Then I saw a little girl come out of the room, and she was crying. Her father said, "I begged you not to go in." The little girl didn't answer, and they both walked straight past me. I went to the door where I had watched them both come out.

There was a man standing there. He looked to be in a nightgown. He said to me, "Don't go in there. You will never come out." I asked him why. He told me to look in but not open the door. I realised it was a morgue. He asked, "What are you doing here?" I told him I did not know. I asked him what he was doing there, and he said he was waiting for someone. I asked, "Who?" And he said, "Everyone." I asked him what he meant, and he said, "Don't you know?" I said no. He replied, "Only the dead come here."

I said, "I'm not dead." He said, "Look into the glass. Do you see your reflection?" I said no. He just looked at me and smiled. I looked down at my hands and my feet and touched my body, and everything seemed to be okay.

He smiled and left. I did not know what to think, so I went back to the lift and waited for someone to press the buttons to go down. Then someone pressed number two, and I thought I would get off and look around.

There were lots of people walking around; some were nurses, and some were visitors, but nobody seemed to see me or hear me when I asked about my mother and father.

Then I met that man again, and he said, "Are you still here?"I said, "I must stay here until I know what is going on."He said, "If you want to know what happened, then you must go to the basement and look through your paperwork." I asked, "Why?" He told me that I would understand. "I will show you where to go." He came with me.

I went towards the lift, but he said no, this way. We went down the steps to the basement. There were rows and rows of boxes. He told me to look for one that had my name on it. I looked at him with questions.

He said, "Never mind, give me your name." "Burrows", I replied. He started to walk down one side of the boxes. He said, "Look for the B, as in your name." Then he called out, "Don't worry, I've got it." We stood there looking at the box, and then he said, "Now, this is where it gets hard. I need you to concentrate." I asked what for, and he said, "To get the bloody box down, of course."

I looked at him and said, "Why don't we just lift it down?" He replied, "You go for it", and gave me that smirking smile again. I lifted my hands up to the box, but nothing happened. My hands seemed to go straight through the box. I asked him what was wrong. He said, "You're dead, of course; that's what's wrong. Let me show you what an expert can do." He closed his eyes and told me to concentrate on the box as if we were going to lift it down.

Then the box started to move, and down it came. He smiled and said, "We would make a good team." The next thing was the lid. He said, "Just think of seeing yourself lifting the lid up." I did, but nothing happened. He said, "You must have patience." And off came the lid. The paperwork came filtering out of the box one paper at a time until there were five pieces of paper in front of us. He said, "This is your death certificate. I'm sorry to say that you died first. Your father died two days later, and your Mother died not long after him." I said, "How?" He said, "I don't bloody know. You must know." He said, "Think what your last thought was." I thought and thought and could not remember.

Then I remembered the plane crash. Oh my God! Everyone was being thrown around; there was a lot of screaming, and people were all over each other, not being able to stand or sit. Seats were being ripped out, and I remember my head getting caught and calling out for my Mother. He said, "Well, now you know." I sat there and cried. He said, "You must start looking towards the future."

I shouted hysterically, "What future? I'm bloody dead!" "Now, now", he said, "that's no kind of language for a young lady." He seemed to blow on the paperwork, and it landed back in the box. He closed his eyes, and the box went back to where we got it from.

Then he sat by me and said, "We have to work together to get you to the other side."

I said, "What another side?"

He said, "Where your mother and father are."

I said, "They are bloody dead!"

He said, "If you say that once more, I will clip you around the head. And if you think I'm joking, then you wait and see."

Then he said, "Come on now, let's go." I followed him. We left the hospital and went to sit by the water's edge.

He said, 'You must have missed your connection. Think of what you were thinking of in your last minutes.'

I remembered thinking, will I ever see Mother again? "That's it," he said. "Well, not exactly. I was mad with Mother just before. I said I will never go with them again for as long as I live."

He just looked at me. "We have to find someone that can take you over," I asked him. How did it work? He told me that you have to want it with all of your soul and much more. You will have to build it up, and it's like building a lot of wishes and stacking them on top of each other. "No more questions," he said. I thought of what he said, but I did not understand. I think he knew that also. He said, "Let's go home and get something to eat." I said, "I thought we were dead?" He said, "What has that got to do with it.?" I shrugged my shoulders and didn't say anything.

I suppose you can say we wished for a hot dog, and there it was, and a Coca-Cola and anything else we wished to eat. It's funny, but when we wanted to sit down, there seemed to be a bench close by. If we wanted to water, a water fountain would come into view. We never seemed to want for anything.

But I did notice that nobody wanted to talk to us, and I was getting a little fed up with people passing by and ignoring us. I asked, "What's going on?" He said, "People don't see us." It felt like weeks and months, but my new friend said it was only hours.

It was getting boring. I tried to play with the children, but no one saw me. He said, "Have you thought any more of the other side?" I said, no, not really. "Well, you better have because I'm not going to babysit you all the time. I have to do other things." I said, "Why don't you want to go to the other side?" He said, "This is my job. To look out for people like you." When I asked why, he replied, "No more questions."

He told me to lie down on the grass, close my eyes, and think of my mother and father. Think of all the good things that we had together and the love they both gave me. Then I remembered them holding me and telling me how they missed me. My heart was so sad that every thought I had went down to my feet, and for one lonely moment, I cried out. I felt a little different lying there. Then I heard a voice say, "Hold my hand", and I remember trying to reach out for this person's hand.

Then, all of a sudden, I felt this warm hand, and I wanted to feel more. The voice kept saying to me, "Hold on tight." I did, with every strength that I possessed. The voice kept talking to me about my mother and father. I told her all about what had happened. I truly loved them both, and I wish I was with them. She told me to close my eyes and think of my mother's smile. I did, and straight away, I felt this lovely, warm feeling coming over me and the beautiful smell of flowers. Then, this beautiful lady came just behind her. She kept on calling my name, and I knew that I was in my mother's arms once more.

17. The Calling

It was peaceful sitting there. The sun was warm, and I'd nearly finished my netting. It had to be repaired so my son and I could go out fishing. I leaned back and stretched my aching back. The aches and pains seemed to be getting worse as I was getting older. One at a time, I stretched out my legs so they didn't fall asleep. I looked out at the beautiful blue yonder. The sea was just turning, and in an hour or so, it would start to get dark.

I leaned back a little more, and my mind started to wander. At that moment, I felt a light blow around my ears. I gently put my hand to my ear and thought of my lovely wife, Guilder. She told me a long time ago that if I ever needed her, she would blow gently in my ear.

I have thought of that moment many times. Thinking of the first time I met my lovely Guilder, how beautiful she was, standing there in front of the drapery shop. I knew I would love her until the day I died.

She had long brown hair, the type of hair you wanted to touch, the bluest eyes you just wanted to look into, and her smile, how it captivated you. She turned slowly and looked my way. I turned away and thought, one day, she will be my wife.

As I slowly walked away, I heard my father calling me; it was time to climb aboard. My father had been fishing all of his life, as had my father's father. I was used to the sea, and I loved being there with my father. As we slowly left the shore behind, I heard someone call my name, "James!" I looked back to the shore, and there she was, waving to me.

My heart took a flip; it was my beautiful Guilder. I waved back with all my heart.

The journey took seven hours, and from the moment we left, I was counting the minutes to get back. When I arrived, it was dark, and the winds were coming in very strong.

I left my father and walked quickly to where I remembered my Guilder standing. I stood where she stood, and I felt a great belonging. It was two months later when we saw each other again.

This time, she was walking towards me. I prayed that she would stop and talk to me again. My heart did a flip. She stood in front of me and asked, "Did you have a good trip, James?" I stumbled forward and finally said, "Yes." Then I asked if she would care to walk with me. She said, "Yes." We strolled along, passing all the friends that we had known all of our lives, but we didn't see them; our minds were on each other. Would I dare reach out and hold her hand? No, it may be too soon. So we just strolled along together, talking about everything and anything.

But the most important thing was being by her side. We were coming to the part of the road where I had to say goodbye, and this was where she would have to leave me. As her house was just around the corner, we bid our farewells, and I asked her if I could see her again.

She smiled and said, "Yes." We were to meet again on Friday, but when I went to meet her, she was not there.

I waited, but she did not come. I thought I would walk down the lane to see if she was there. It was a lane that all the villagers used to walk down to the beach. I saw a friend on the way. He stopped me and said, "Did you hear the news? One of the boats didn't come back." "Which one?" I asked. "Old Ted's boat." Then he said what everyone else had said, "The old boat needed to be retired; it's too old."

But my thoughts went to Guilder. What will she be going through? I shook his hand, thanked him, and ran all the way to Guilder's house. She was on the veranda crying. I ran to her, put my arms around her, and held her until she stopped crying. I told her everything was going to be okay and I would look after her. You see, Ted was the only family Guilder had left. All her other family were gone.

Friends started to leave, so I told her to lie down and try to get some sleep. She begged me, "Please don't go." I never did. I stayed by her bedside and watched her fall asleep.

We married in the spring, and we never parted for forty years, and then I lost her to ill health. But I knew she was there with me; I knew she would never leave my side.

The sun was getting warmer, and I started to feel uncomfortable. I thought how much longer it would be before I could see my lovely Guilder again. My chest hurts now. Then I heard my Guilder calling me. "Are you ready, my darling? Come hold my hand. Once more, we will walk together. I love you so."I felt her hand in mine, and nothing mattered any more.

18. While You Were Sleeping

I walked down to the small garden where I'd been many times before. I opened my sandwich, placed the cup of coffee by the side of me, and started to take a bite. I was not really interested in eating it, so I put the sandwich back in the wrapper. There wasn't a lot to see sitting there, only parts of the hospital buildings.

I leaned back, closed my eyes, and thought of the last time we spent together. We'd gone on a week's trip. We had not been away together for a long time. I thought back and said to myself, "That was the best week I ever had." I looked at my watch and realised I had been sitting there for twenty minutes. I picked up my sandwich and my coffee and took the lift back upstairs.

I walked back into his room and sat by the side of the bed. I looked at my son and thought, will he ever wake up? I'd brought my knitting; I was knitting him a new jumper. It was blue, but I thought I would add some yellow to brighten the jumper up. I was getting fed up of knitting the same things day after day.

The nurse came in and checked Alan, smiled at him and, said that everything was okay, and walked away.

I don't know why, but I just cried. I put the knitting down and started to talk to Alan as I had done many times, but this time, I told him about when he was a little boy.

I told him about the first house that we moved into and that his father, Barry, was a baker. He would bring special biscuits home for him. I told him how much his father loved him from the minute he was born. I told him how special he was to both of us. I told him about his first birthday and the excitement. I told him about his first day in school and how I hated not seeing him all day. I was the last to leave the school and the first to arrive. I was so proud of my son.

Not long after his fourteenth birthday, his father got sick and a year after that, he passed away. He was a very good husband and father, and I missed him every day.

The nurse came in and asked if I wanted something to drink. I said, "A cup of tea would be fine, thank you." I started to talk to my son again. I told him about the last week that we'd spent together, the beautiful sights that we both admired. I asked him if he remembered losing his cap when we were on the boat. I felt myself smiling, and for the first time, I felt happy.

I took my son's hand as I told him about the little dog that kept pulling on the leg of his trousers. Then I stopped and sat down. I remembered my son singing as he drove the car, and I remembered looking ahead and seeing the truck coming towards us. The screams, the screeching of the tyres, and the ambulance man trying to revive my son.

I thought, can life end so quickly? I sat back and thought, if my son dies, then I want to die also. I'd lost the best husband a person could have. I've got the best son a mother could have. If my son is taken away, then I no longer want to live. I must have spoken those words out loud because just then, the nurse came in and said, "Are you okay?" I said, "Yes." She said, "I think you should talk to someone." I said, "Not today, thank you."

I took the tea from her and sat back down. I placed the tea on the bedside cabinet and stood up, and anger came rushing through me. I beat on my son's chest and shouted with all my might, "Don't you dare leave me! If you go, I will go! Don't even think of leaving me!"

At that moment, a bell started to ring. Something else happened, and I fell to the floor.

I woke up in a hospital bed, and the Doctor was standing over me. He said, "We've done a check, and everything is okay, but we would like you to rest here for twenty-four hours." Then, with a glint in his eye, he said, "I don't know what you did, but I think you just performed a miracle on your son." I asked him what he meant. He said, "Your son has shown signs of coming out of unconsciousness. His eyes are starting to flicker, and his breathing is getting better. If everything goes well, we will take you to see him in a moment." I could not believe what I was hearing. The Doctor winked at me and walked away.

I could not wait for someone to come and get me. I was already in the room, sitting by the side of the bed, holding his hand. For one brief moment, I felt a slight twitch in his hand. I called the nurse and told her; she said that his reflexes were starting to work again. At that moment, my son opened his eyes briefly. I couldn't say anything through the tears that were falling and the sorrow that was emptying out of my heart.

The nurse had to ask me to sit back down, or she would have to send me out of the room. I sat down immediately.

The doctor came in and looked at my son and said, "He's going to be okay." I could not think of a thing to say, but I was so excited. Then the doctor turned around to me and said, "Kate, God must have heard your prayer." I smiled and asked, "Which one?"

The nurse said I had to go and get some rest, but I was too excited. I said, "No, thank you. I've been here all the time he's been asleep, and I am sure as hell not going to leave him now when he wakes up." She smiled at me and left the room.

The nurses were very good to me. They gave me a camp bed in the room to use, but I just lay there, not daring to sleep in case my son woke up and wanted to see me.

Everything happened so fast after that. The morning came, and breakfast was served. The nurse said, "You can stay on one condition. If you don't eat, you don't stay." So I agreed and ate my hard-boiled eggs and toast, all the time watching for anything different from my son.

As I put the plates back on the tray, I looked at my son and saw him, for the first time, open his eyes wide and look around. I threw my arms around him and said, "I'm here." He searched for my hand. I took hold of it, and I could feel the strength coming into his body.

The doctor was there by his bedside again and said, "I'm going to try and take his mouthpiece out and see if he can manage." Ten minutes later, my son was saying, "Mum, I'm going to be okay." He fell asleep at that moment, and six hours later, he woke up a different person.

He was still being fed by tubes, but he was communicating with everyone now. Then he asked, "How long have I been here?" I said, "Three months, six days, and ninety-two minutes." He looked at me, smiled, and said, "And how long have you been here, Mother?" The nurse replied, "Three months, six days, and ninety-two minutes." We all laughed together.

My son had been awake now for a week, and we had been talking about the accident and what had happened. He could not remember much at all, so I filled him in. I asked him if he remembered anything else.

He said, "It's strange, but I heard you talking now and again about my school and my father. I heard the nurse asking if you would like a cup of tea. But most of all, I heard your knitting needles clicking all the time you were knitting.

I felt comfort in the sound. I remembered you knitting when I was young, so the sound of the needles stayed with me."

I told the young nurse what Allen had said, and she said it was strange to think that he was unconscious yet still aware of things happening.

around him. I thought for a moment and walked out of the room and up the stairs towards the other rooms I knew very well. I'd visited there when my son was sick. Three or four people were in the room, similar to my son, who had never woken up.

I went along to each and every one of them and told them, "You are not forgotten. You must find your way back. Listen to the memories of your soul and tell them it's not your time. Find a way like my son did."

I walked away from the last one, and the Sister came over and said, "That was a very nice thing that you did." I said to her that once a week, I would come back and say the same things over and over again until, one by one, these young men woke up.

She smiled at me and said, "Then I'm looking forward to seeing you in the future." I walked back down the stairs to my son's room, and the world changed once more. I was a mother, and once more, I had a son.

19. A Beautiful Smile

I am walking along the side of a huge pond. It's very cold, and I wrap my coat further around me. I am walking along an old path by the pond where the water flows gently into a weir. Not today; it's frozen over with ice. I looked across, and it was even colder than I could have imagined. I look down at my feet; they are so cold, and then I see a face looking up at me through the ice below.

I noticed that it was a man with a beautiful smile, but he was completely under the ice, just lying there. I think what I can do. Then I heard my guide say, "Put your hand on the ice where his face is." I gently lay my hand on the ice, and amazingly, the ice started to melt all around him. With a huge effort, I drag his body from the ice and hold him in my arms.

I carefully lift a lock of his hair from his eyes and hold him even closer to me. He still had a smile on his face, and then he opened his eyes and said, "I could not find her." I asked who. "My wife", he says. Then he tells me with great sadness how his wife had died and how he misses her.

"Two long years I waited", he tells me, "then I couldn't wait any longer. I walked out into the middle of the ice with a brick in my hand, and I hit the ice with all my loneliness, again and again, until the ice broke. I went straight to the bottom, and I was smiling because I knew it would not be long before I saw my lovely wife again. But when I did see her, it was only for a brief moment as I passed her by. I could not stop; it was the pull of time."

I asked what he meant. He said, "I have been waiting thirty-two years for you to come." I was confused but realised because he had taken his own life, he then had to wait until the time was right for him to move on, as time itself was forgiving.

I helped him up, and we knew we must walk the ice together for the last time. As we walked further in, he loosened his coat and let it drop to the ground. Then, he loosened his tie and said, "I can feel the warmth of the sun on my face."

I said yes. He smiled at me and said, "Thank you for being there for me." He walked away, seeing the only thing he ever wanted to see. He was smiling.

20. Waiting For Mummy

When we first met, I was surprised to see things had not changed in thirty-two years. There was a little girl between nine and eleven, sitting in a train carriage with her nose pressed onto the large glass window, the only one I could see still not shattered. I spoke to the little girl from the aisle of the carriage. I asked if I could please sit by her, and she replied without taking her eyes from the window, "Yes, but not next to me because that is where my Mummy sits, and she's coming back for me."

I sat there for a few minutes and then asked, "Where is your Mummy?"

"Mummy said she would not belong. She just went to find my Daddy, and I must not move from the seat until she gets back." The little girl still did not take her eyes from the window.

I told her my name and asked her what her name was. "Wendy", she replied, still not taking her eyes from the window. I sat there for about five more minutes. I then asked if she liked butterflies. She said yes, and then I told her there was a beautiful butterfly right on the end of her nose.

She jumped away from the window and tried to see the butterfly at the end of her nose. I told her to put her finger out in front of the butterfly, and it would land on her finger. I said if she was really good, she would see two beautiful butterflies on her finger. With that, she let out an excited little scream as she saw two butterflies on her finger.

Then she turned and looked at me for the first time. I smiled and said that if she closed her eyes, she would see lots and lots. She closed her eyes and then asked, "Can I open my eyes?" I said yes, and she laughed to see all the beautiful butterflies around her. I let this go on for about ten minutes and then said to her, "How many did you count?" She said, "Thousands and thousands", with so much laughter.

I knew I had to get her off the train to release her from the promise she had made to her mother thirty-two years ago. I told her that I had seen the most beautiful butterfly of her size. I asked her if she wanted to see it too. She said, "What about Mummy? Will she be cross?" I told her I believed her Mummy was there too, looking at this beautiful butterfly.

She held my hand with so much trust as we walked out of the train together. A lady with coloured wings came and gently picked up my little friend so carefully, and just before they walked through the beautiful mist, she turned and waved to

me and said, "I did see the most beautiful

butterfly, didn't I?" I smiled and said, "Yes, darling, you did."

21. The Looking Glass

I hate springtime. I look down, pick up my glass and try to straighten my hair. There's not much left of it anymore; there's not much left of anything except for a lot of wrinkles. I don't recognise the woman looking back at me; I never did.

It was in the springtime, and my mind slipped back. I remember waving to my husband and children. I'd never had a holiday.

For the first time, I was going on a walking holiday with my friend Sally. David was fourteen, and Shelley was twelve. I did not want to leave them, but I had been quite sick.

Everyone said I needed a holiday and because I love to go bushwalking, my friend said she had seen the holiday on special; would I like to go? I said yes, and then she told me it was in Canada for two weeks.

I could not believe it. I had never set foot off the farm since the day I was born. But Marty, my husband, said, "You will enjoy it all the more by aeroplane than by driving holiday."

Well, it seemed that everyone had made up my mind. I loved my husband dearly and my children. He always told me that I was the most beautiful girl in the world. I smiled and remembered when we first met. It was at one of those balls, you know, the one where single wives and daughters get together with single fathers and sons.

I had never been to one before, but Mother said it would be good for me to get out of the house.

So Mother took me. I had just turned eighteen. I had never seen so many people under one roof. We had it in Mr Black's shed; there must have been sixty people. The music was so loud, and everyone was jigging about.

I went to look for Mother but couldn't see her. I had to walk into the crowd to find her.

Someone caught my hand and said, "Let's dance Beautiful." I didn't know how to dance, and I never considered myself beautiful.

For the next six months, we were a couple, and he always introduced me as his beautiful Dotty. My name was Dorothy, but no one called me that; it was always Dotty.

I heard a car pull up outside the house, and my friend Sally called, "Let's go, or we will miss the plane." There was so much excitement.

My husband and children crowded around me, hugging and kissing me farewell. Then I was in the car waving to everyone. The plane was on time, and off we went. Sally was so excited; she talked all the way there.

We arrived, and the bellboy took our luggage up to the room. It was quite cosy, but it was not home. I was already missing my family, but it was late in the evening now, and it was time to sleep.

The following morning, we were woken by a bell ringing, telling us it was breakfast.

There was so much to do that time just flew by. Two days before we were due to fly home, a friend that we had met while on holiday said they were putting on a special walking treat for us to the mountains.

Now, I thought, this is something I look forward to. We have hills back home, but not mountains like these. We had to wear special shoes and clothing, but we enjoyed every moment.

We left at six-thirty in the morning to start the climb. Everything went well until it was time to come back down, and for some unknown reason, everything went wrong.

There was a landslide above us; we could not get out of the way in time. I remember calling for Sally just before the rock seemed to open up and swallow me. I don't know how long I lay there, but I knew every part of my body was aching.

One of my legs was trapped. I seemed to be in some kind of a crevice. I turned around. I could see small lights behind me. I called out, but nobody answered. I kept calling and calling, but still, nobody heard my calls.

I don't know how long I was there, but later, I was told it was four days. I was conscious of the light and tried to move towards it. I pulled on some of the loose rocks. The gap was getting bigger.

God knows why I hadn't been crushed. I crawled out and lay there for a while. Then I felt someone turning me over, lifting my head and giving me water. I was so thirsty I wanted to drink it all, but the man pulled the drink bottle away from me. He told me I would be sick if I drank too fast. The man turned away from me and said he was sorry.

Everything started to fall into place. I asked about my face. I was in so much pain. He said he had sent for help, and it was on its way.

It was only a small village, and the helpers were strange but good people. They carried me in a handmade stretcher made of bamboo.

I don't remember getting there or the days that followed, but I do know now I was ill for six months. My face had been so badly damaged that my cheekbones were broken, and my face was disfigured. No one would let me look into anything that would reflect my face.

Then, one day, I went to the brook to look into the water, and I could not believe what looked back at me. I screamed with all the pain in the world and screamed and screamed until, finally, I didn't have anything left in me to scream.

Time was going by now. For the first time, we had a stranger come to visit the villagers. He was from the village on the other side of the mountain. He said a doctor and nurse were coming in to see the villagers in the next two days.

The woman, who was called the elder, said it was time for me to seek help. This life here was not for me; they didn't mean to hurt my feelings, but it was best for me.

For the next two days, I walked back through the mountain with Bunya. He didn't speak much, but I knew he was worried about me. We arrived in the village in the late afternoon.

Some of the people looked at me and smiled. Some of them, the younger ones, turned their heads away. One of the village people took my hand and took me to the tent that had been made up for the doctor and nurse.

The nurse took one look at me, said, "Oh my God!" and put her hands to her face. I didn't know what to do.

The doctor took me to one side and said, "Sit down, please." He asked me my name, but with everything going on, I did not want to talk. He made me a cup of tea and told me they were flying back the following day. Would I like to go with them?

I said yes, but that night, as I lay in the bed, I thought, I don't want my husband and children to see me like this. I decided I would get help before I went home.

I realised it must be nearly a year since I'd seen my family. I have missed them every day since the accident. What would they think when they saw me again? Would they even recognise me? I didn't know, and it was too hard to think about it. I decided I would wait until after the operation.

The doctor said that there were a lot of things that could be done today through plastic surgery, but I was not looking forward to it. I had never been in a hospital in my life.

I finally dropped off to sleep. When I woke up, the tent had already been pulled down, and the doctor and nurse were ready to leave. We walked back towards the river, and there was a small aeroplane waiting for us with its engine running. We quickly climbed aboard, and the plane took off.

My memories go back to the last time I flew, and tears come running down my cheeks. I looked out of the window so no one could see me crying. Two hours later, we landed and were taken by car to the big hospital. The nurse took me to a small room with a shower and toilet.

I asked if I could have a shower; it had been a long time since I'd been in civilisation. She left me, and I quickly got into the shower. It felt so good I didn't want to get out.

The memories again come flooding back, and I'm in my own shower back on the farm. I can hear the children laughing in the background. I could hear Sally shouting my name, and then all of a sudden, I remembered Sally. What happened to Sally? Oh God! What happened to Sally?

Nobody mentioned the other people that were with me. Nobody said anything, and I never asked.

It took all my strength to go back day by day. Why did I not remember what happened to my friend Sally? What happened to her? Did someone find her, too?

I don't remember anything. I shook my head from side to side, trying so desperately to remember, but nothing came to me. I turned the shower off and quickly got dressed. I ran out into the corridor and asked for Nurse Gabby.

That was her nickname; you could understand why, as she never stopped talking.

Another nurse told me she had gone for lunch, but I would catch her at the outside door if I were quick. I ran through the corridors, and yes, she was just leaving.

I said, "What happened to my friend and the other people?" She looked at me with concern and said, "Everyone died except you. For some unknown reason, you fell into a crevice which allowed you to breathe and to survive."

I turned slowly around and walked back to my room, fell on the bed, and cried my heart out. Later on that night, the doctor came and said, "You must eat. You will need all the strength you have for the next few months. We will get you looking like Mona Lisa again." He smiled, but it didn't seem so important now that my friends were all dead.

The next few weeks were a daze for me. I was prodded and pulled around. I had already had my first operation, and the second one was tomorrow.

I tried to keep my spirits up, looking forward to returning home. I had not told anyone my name. For anyone who asked, I begged them, "Please don't tell anyone I'm here." I think they all understood and kept my secret.

I was known as the lady in bed fourteen. Time went by; another six months and more operations. Every time I looked into the looking glass, I still did not recognise the woman looking back at me.

As time went by, I faced the fact that by now, my family would have started a new life. The grief that I gave them had long gone.

I left the hospital soon after the last operation and met one of the old nurses that I got used to. She invited me to stay and help her with people who could not afford medical assistance.

She'd taught me how to put bandages on, take temperatures, and do most things the nurse would do, and I started to enjoy my new life.

Then, one day, my friend asked me if I could go to the library for her and look up one of the death notices for one of the patients.

I went to the library the following day and found what I was looking for. As I was turning the machine off, something caught my eye. It was the anniversary of the death of my friend. I quickly got it back on the screen and saw the funeral notices of all the people.

I saw my husband and two children standing with all the other families, and my heart went out to them. I went back into research and found a marriage proposal with my husband's name on it. It gave me a shock and a jolt, but I had to remember it had been six years since the accident, and I think I knew I would never go back.

I could not expect my family to love me the way I was, and my husband was so proud of his beautiful wife. What would he think now there were too many scars?

I thought I'd recognised the name, but the accident had wiped out a lot of the memories, thank God.

Time went by, and I went back to the library to keep in touch with my family. The weddings were the worst. My daughter's wedding and the pictures were also there. I had learned to live in a world of numbness; nobody got in, and I couldn't get out.

I've lived with my decision. I wished I had had the strength to go back, but I didn't; God only knows I'd tried, but I'm happy for the memories.

My friend passed away some twenty years ago and left me her house. The job she trained me for brings in the money. It's not much, but I don't need much.

People are happy to accept me the way I am, and for that, I am grateful.

Many years have passed, and I've watched my children grow up through the papers. I've given up the memory of ever seeing them again. The doctor helped me a long time ago to change my name; he understood what it meant to me.

So I gently put down the looking glass and turned around to look at what I didn't know. I managed to climb onto the bed and lay down. I closed my eyes, and once again, I was with my husband and my children.

The memories now seemed very strong, and I heard my friend Sally calling me once again. "Let go; they are only memories; let them go."

I called out and said, "I can't!" She held her hand out and said, "Let's do the memories together." I reached out to hold her hand, and as I did, I let go of all the earthly promises.

The next thing I knew, we were reminiscing about our lives together, sailing higher and higher. For the first time, I smiled and let go of all the hurt and told her how I'd missed her.

22. A Christmas Carol

Another Christmas was coming closer. As I placed the last Christmas ball on the tree, I heard my son calling. It was a long time since he had called me Mother.

He had grown up to be a fine young man, and I remember him saying, "I don't want to call you Mother any more; I will now call you Angie." I took a small curtsey and said, "Thank you, kind Sir." But that was a long time ago.

My husband and I had our son later in life. He was always very special. We had been married for ten years, and we thought we would never have a child. So, it was a great surprise when I found out I was pregnant. I could not believe what the doctor was saying. I was so excited I ran out of the doctor's office to tell my husband.

"We're pregnant! We're pregnant!" I shouted for the whole world to hear. Everyone in the office stopped and looked, but I did not care. My husband came running out and asked, "Are you sure?" I looked back at him and said, "Yes, darling, I'm three months pregnant."

We both laughed at each other, and all of my husband's friends in the office came to congratulate us.

I finally returned to my senses and realised that I was still wearing the doctor's gown I had put over my clothes. I walked back, got into the car, drove back to the surgery, passed over the gown to the receptionist and apologised. She smiled and said she understood.

I was so excited that I did not want to go home straight away, so I thought I would go and see a friend of mine. She knew straight away when she opened the door that something exciting was happening. She said, "Come in, I've got the kettle on. I must have known you were going to call."

I could hardly restrain myself as I jumped up and down and shouted out, "I'm pregnant!" She sat down on the stool and asked, "How? When?" I replied, "How, the usual way, and when? I'm three months gone."

She took me in her arms, and we both jumped for joy. After all the excitement, we sat down and planned what we were going to do for the new baby.

She said, "You must get the beautiful pram that we were looking at a few weeks ago." I said, "That was a strange thing for us to be looking at then." She giggled and said, "Maybe it was a sign."

After that day, every day was a blessing. I woke up and felt my tummy to make sure I was not dreaming.

Then, the big day arrived, and we were handed a beautiful baby boy. We named him Luke, after my husband's father. My husband had loved his father, but he had died before my husband had the chance to get to know him. He always said if he was lucky enough to have a son, he would name him Luke.

Luke grew up doing very well in school and said he would like to be a doctor one day. I asked, "Why a doctor?"

He told me that the other day, he had gone with his friend to visit his friend's mother in the hospital. While he was waiting, he walked around the wards and thought, I could do better with these people. I want to study and make them well. But I also want to let them know that they are loved by everyone they come in contact with.

He said, "I saw a lot of people sitting or lying on their own. Some of them wanted to hold my hand, so I held their hand." I knew my son would make a good doctor.

So, my son started studying. He was studying very well, and then we heard that the war had broken out, and they were calling young men up by their birthdays.

Every day, we would listen to the radio station, hoping and praying that his birthday was not called out.

Then, one day, it happened, and we could not do anything but let him go. That was the day he decided to stop calling me Mother and call me by my name, Angie. Angela was my full name, but my son said he preferred to call me Angie. No one else was allowed to do so. So, Angie, it was.

Nine months into the war, my son had been injured. They said that he was being sent home with honours. He had placed himself in danger while trying to rescue three of his mates.

One had died through injuries, and he had brought the other two back, but in doing so, he had been badly injured himself.

They did not say what his injuries were, so we were shocked when the cab turned up, and my son was helped out and then placed in a wheelchair. He had lost both of his legs. The shock was so great that I collapsed into my husband's arms.

Luke said he was so sorry that I had to find out this way, but he did not want anyone else breaking the news of his injuries to the family. I slowly pulled myself together and said how sorry I was.

But later, I found that his legs were not all that was missing from my son. He had lost the gentleness, and the spark had gone out of those eyes.

I looked at him day after day and watched my son giving up on life. My husband and I talked to the Group Captain about our son and asked what we could do. He replied, "I'm sorry, but only time will tell. He had to watch his mates die, one after another." We both looked at each other and said nothing.

Once more, I found myself placing the last Christmas ball on the tree. I stood down and looked back. I heard my son calling me. I went towards the bedroom that he had grown up in.

He had lost his hair, and my heart went out to him. He said, "Mother, thank you for always being there for me." I smiled and said, "Why are you telling me this?"

He said, "Sometimes we leave things too late to say, and I felt that I should say what is in my heart tonight." I wanted to scream out, but I was afraid to break the moment. I sat by his bedside and listened to what he said.

He told me things I did not want to hear about the war and his friends, but I sat there and listened. I looked at his face and saw how tired he really was. I reached out for his hand, bent over, and kissed his forehead. At that moment, I heard carolers singing, and my son asked, "Please open the door, Mother, so I can hear them."

I walked to the door and opened it, and seven young people were there. I asked them, "Could you sing a special song for my son?"Some of them knew my Luke, and I know the song that they sang was especially for him. I walked back to his bedside and held his hand.

We both listened to the Christmas carol together, and just before it finished, I turned and looked at Luke, but I knew he was gone. I sat there for a moment longer and then thought, I'd better thank the young people for singing. I walked back to where Luke was lying, and I swear I could see an Angel picking him up and holding him very carefully in her arms, and then they were both gone.

I felt a huge sadness in my heart, then thought of my son in the arms of such a beautiful Angel; I thought he really must have been a special boy.

23.The Medium

I stood there, as I had done many times before, but this time it was different. I looked into the audience, and I could hear someone crying. Asking, "Please tell them to let me go. I'm tired, and I need to go forward. I've tried in so many ways to tell them I'm okay. I love them both so very much, but they don't listen. Day by day, I'm getting weaker and weaker, and the time will come when I will no longer have the energy to cross over. How can you tell your parents to let you go? I have watched them since the day I died. Their grieving is tearing me apart. I would like to tell you what it is like here when you can no longer communicate with someone on the Earth plane."

JUST THE TOUCH

"I want to explain. I reach out and touch Mother, but it's not an earthly experience. When you touch someone on an earth plane, you immediately get a response. When you cry, you immediately get a response back, and the response you get you can act upon because you still have the ability to feel, to see, and to hear.

"Once these precious things have been taken away, you are left with the vibrations, and in this new world, we need vibrations. That is not the same as being on Earth. How can I tell my parents that my heart aches because I cannot tell them I love them and how I am feeling? If you get the chance to hear my call, I beg of you, with all my heart, please let me go.

I will never forget you, and I know you will never forget me."But this heartache goes on and on with no end. I have a new beginning, and at this moment, that is all I have. So please, let me go. Just think of me as going on a long holiday and putting me on a boat and waving goodbye.

"Knowing also that we will see each other again and, when you think of me, then think of me as going on a journey and the journey that one day will bring me back to you and as a stronger person.

"I will always love you as you both love me. Please, let me go."

24. The Gift

I was given the gift of communicating with the dead. This Is The Truth, The Whole, And Nothing But The Truth. I have honestly been there, and I was told to go back by the angel Of Mercy and that my life would change within two years.

It did change, and I kept my promise, and they kept theirs. I promised to listen to people from the other side telling me their stories of their life and Death experiences. I have listened to hundreds of their stories, filled 23 books, and won three awards In America.

If you have crossed over and been given a second chance at life, I believe it was for a reason. Mine was listening to the other side's stories to help people understand. Not only life But also Death. I was a person of no belief, But I came back with a miracle of understanding both worlds.

Thank You for Reading Their Book

I would like to thank the people who have read my books and hope that you enjoyed them. Those of you who have read my other books will understand that these people come from all walks of life and from different cultures, backgrounds and levels of education.

Please keep this in mind when you read my books: these people are here to tell their stories, not to explain.

I love sitting and listening to them. At first, I used to think how sad the stories were, but now I realize that every story I write educates me on how to understand the living and the dead. Some of the stories you will be able to relate to because somewhere in your life, you have had similar experiences. Please remember, these are their stories, and I am here to help them cross over.' I hope that there will be many more stories to come. Once again, thank you for reading my books.

The Ouija Board

Be careful whom you invite into your home; you may not get to get rid of them. All the places that I have been to. And all my understanding does not always protect me from the empty energies from beyond. Our only control is our guides.

This is what I believe. I believe many lost souls are out there, not knowing or understanding how to connect to someone with the ability and why they are still here; it is a Catch-22 for them. They do not always know where they are, about the other side or the understanding of death.

Once again, I ask you to be careful whom you invite into your home. They may not want to move on.

From The American Readers Club

Pam McCagh gives readers a nuanced view of Death and confirms its inevitable presence in our lives. The author clears many doubts surrounding the myth of what happens after we die by exploring Death in a way that helps readers appreciate life in general.

Death and its facts have always been surrounded by a lot of arguments and controversies, but the author teaches us to look at it in a different light altogether and embrace what is inevitable.

In this interesting book, the author exposes many myths surrounding Death, angels, crossing over, and much more with the help of the stories that have been told to her by the beautiful souls around her.

All the stories have been written by memories, which also reveals the author's ability to connect with the spirit world. Her spiritual powers make the stories genuine and effective.

The book connects us between the two spectrums and helps us to have a better understanding of life,

Death, and consciousness. It is an assimilation of spirituality teemed with science, and the author has made it easier for readers to comprehend the theme.

The stories help readers to have a better understanding of the larger picture and cosmic law.

It is a fascinating book that raises your awareness surrounding Death, and it helps us look at the inevitable from a different perspective and with acceptance.

I would like to take this opportunity to thank Pamela for giving me the opportunity to read just one of the books. I know that there are many more.

NEVER FORGET TO TELL SOMEONE YOU LOVE THEM, AS YOU MAY NOT GET ANOTHER CHANCE.

Thank You For Reading Their Book
And Reading Their Stories
Pam McCagh

Printed in Dunstable, United Kingdom

69120235R00117